P9-BYM-067

THE ROUGH GUIDE to

iPods & iTunes

6th Edition

ROUGH GUIDES

www.roughguides.com

Credits

The Rough Guide to iPods & iTunes

Text, design and layout:
Peter Buckley and Duncan Clark
Proofreading: Susanne Hillen
Production: Rebecca Short

Rough Guides Reference

Director: Andrew Lockett
Editors: Kate Berens, Peter Buckley,
Tracy Hopkins, Matthew Milton,
Joe Staines, Ruth Tidball

Publishing information

This sixth edition published October 2009 by
Rough Guides Ltd, 80 Strand, London, WC2R 0RL
Email: mail@roughguides.com

Distributed by the Penguin Group:
Penguin Books Ltd, 80 Strand, London, WC2R 0RL
Penguin Group (USA), 375 Hudson Street, NY 10014, USA
Penguin Group (Australia), 250 Camberwell Road, Camberwell, Victoria 3124, Australia
Penguin Group (Canada), 90 Eglinton Avenue East, Suite 700, Toronto, Ontario, Canada M4P 2Y3
Penguin Group (New Zealand), Cnr Rosedale and Airborne Roads, Albany, Auckland, New Zealand

Printed and bound in Singapore by SNP Security Printing Pte Ltd

Typeset in Minion and Gill Sans

Back cover image courtesy of Apple Computer UK

The publishers and authors have done their best to ensure the accuracy and currency of all information in
The Rough Guide to iPods & iTunes; however, they can accept no responsibility for any loss or inconvenience
sustained by any reader as a result of its information or advice.

288 pages; includes index

A catalogue record for this book is available from the British Library.

ISBN 13: 978-1-84836-259-8

1 3 5 7 9 8 6 4 2

THE ROUGH GUIDE to

iPods & iTunes

Peter Buckley

www.roughguides.com

Contents

contents

Organizing & playing

Extras

First aid

iPodology

About
this book

Why a book about iPods?

Several years ago, when we first thought of writing this book, we wondered whether there would be enough to say. Apple are famous for making user-friendly products, and iPods and iTunes are particularly intuitive. But once we started talking to people who either already had an iPod or were thinking of buying one, we realized that there was clearly a need. Everyone had a question – "Is the sound quality any good?", "How do I move music between my two computers?", "Is downloading illegal?". Five editions later some of the questions have changed – "How do I convert video formats?", "which are the best apps to download?" – but the need is still there.

So here are a couple of hundred pages of answers, not only covering iPod and iTunes basics, but everything from finding music and video online and choosing the right audio file formats to resurrecting your old vinyl collection and getting it into your pocket. You'll also find a few samples of iPod culture – such as the devoted fans who obsess about their Pods' names and find all manner of bizarre ways to glorify their Apple gadgets. Not everyone is quite that keen, of course, but one thing that all Pod users agree on is that iPods change our relationship to digital media, most especially music. And with the scores of tips and tricks provided in this book, that relationship should be as satisfying as a Bach fugue. Or a Coltrane solo. Or a Missy Elliott a cappella…

Note!

Each new version of iTunes brings a different set of features, and each new iPod model works slightly differently.

This book was written using iTunes 8.1, so if you have something older, be sure to upgrade to the most recent version (see p.40) or many of the functions covered here will be missing. Likewise, if you have something newer (iTunes updates are released every few months), expect to find numerous extras.

As for hardware, this book focuses on the models available in April 2009: the iPod shuffle, iPod nano, iPod classic and iPod touch. Most of what we say will apply to older models, too, though certain features – Notes, Dock connectors, and so on – were only introduced with the third-generation iPods in 2003. Equally, Web browsing features only apply to the iPod touch, and video capability was only bestowed upon the nano with its third generation, released in the autumn of 2007.

The
basics

01

Essential Q&As

Everything you ever wanted to know about iPods and downloading but were afraid to ask

This book should help you get the best from an iPod, from iTunes and from Internet downloading. However, before we get into the nitty-gritty of everything from ripping tracks from vinyl to using the iPod as a hard drive, let's address all those general questions that you've probably already asked yourself (and some that you probably haven't) about the world of MP3 players. You'll find more details on many of these subjects later on.

Basics

What is an iPod?

An iPod is like a cross between a Walkman and the hard drive in a computer (see box below). Instead of playing from cassettes, CDs or other media, an iPod holds music internally as digital data, in just the same way as a computer stores word-processing documents and other files.

iPods aren't unique in this respect: many devices do roughly the same thing. They're collectively known as digital media players or (for reasons soon to be explained) MP3 players. But the iPod – produced by Apple, also known for their Mac range of computers – is by far the most popular of the numerous brands on the market.

Hard drives and flash

These days, most digital music players – such as the iPod nano, iPod shuffle and iPod touch – store their music using "flash" memory: tiny chips of the kind found in digital-camera memory cards. High-capacity digital media players, including the iPod classic, store their music on a hard drive, or "hard disk" – similar to the one found in a standard home computer. Hard drives can store more data, but flash memory is more resistant to being knocked around and is physically smaller (Apple couldn't get the iPod touch that thin with a conventional hard drive).

What can an iPod do?

All iPods can play music imported from CD or downloaded from the Internet. They can do this through earphones, or by being connected to a speaker unit, hi-fi or car stereo.

Recent iPods also allow you to display images and videos. So you can have your digital photo albums with you at all times (a mixed blessing for friends and relatives, admittedly), as well as home movies and even copies of your DVDs. In addition, the iPod touch allows you to access the Internet via Wi-Fi to surf the Web, download music from the iTunes Store and also download apps from the App Store (see p.119), which expand the functionality of the touch and allow you to do everything from play sophisticated video games to make Internet telephone calls using Skype.

On top of all that, you can also use an iPod as a portable hard drive to back up or transfer any kind of computer files. An 120GB iPod, for example, is the equivalent of more than 75,000 floppy disks – enough to back up a huge quantity of documents, emails and photos.

Recent iPods also offer some basic calendars and contacts features. However, only the iPod touch is really useful in this regard, as it allows you to actually *enter* dates and details rather than just displaying information created on your computer.

Furthermore, all iPods can play audiobooks and other spoken-word recordings. Their large capacity makes it practical to store entire texts – so you don't have to make do with the hatchet-job abridgements typically found on cassettes and CDs.

And that's not all. Here are a few other things you can do with an iPod, some of which require a third-party accessory or app…

▶ **Record voice memos** See p.224

▶ **Read news and email on the train** See p.205

▶ **Use an iPod touch as a remote control** See p.241

▶ **Remotely control iTunes over Wi-Fi** See p.241

▶ **Play the guitar** See p.122

▶ **Stitch together a photo panorama** See p.81

▶**Watch your favourite DVDs** See p.184

▶ **Remember what you should be doing** See p.122

▶**Automatically back up key files** See p.245

▶ **Play games** See p.104 & p.122

▶ **Find your way around** See p.207

▶ **Keep a virtual pet** See p.122

▶ **Shave off your beard** See p.265

Why would I want to put my music on an iPod?

There are numerous attractions in putting your music on an iPod or other high-spec digital media player. Compared to other types of personal stereo, they win hands down. For one thing, they can store a huge quantity of music – thousands of albums in some cases – so you can listen to whatever you want, wherever you are. Secondly, since there are no CDs or tapes to carry about, all you have to take with you is a small, self-contained device. Furthermore, iPods (like other personal stereos) can be hooked up to home hi-fis or car stereos, which means you can have your entire music collection instantly accessible at home, at friends' houses, when you're driving – even on holiday.

iPods and iTunes also open up new ways of arranging and listening to your music. You can compile playlists of choice songs – a four-hour upbeat selection for a party, say, or a shorter selection for a walk to work. Or have your player select your music for you, picking tracks randomly from your whole collection or even making selections based on what it thinks you might like.

Is an iPod the best digital media player to buy?

The various members of the iPod family are the best-known digital media players and they have much to recommend them. They're solidly built but small and light. They're reliable and easy to use. They work with the excellent iTunes software (more on this later). There are scores of accessories and piles of extra software available for them. And they're masterpieces of ergonomic and aesthetic design (with the one exception of the grossly misjudged U2 special edition, released in late 2004). However, as with most Apple products, these qualities are reflected in a higher-than-average price.

There are many similar players which lack the wide reputation and minimalist design but which offer more features – such as an integrated radio and longer battery life – for less money. There are many brands out there, among whom the biggest players are Creative Labs (who produce the Zen brand), iRiver, Microsoft (who make Zune players) and Sony. From here on in, this book focuses exclusively on iPods. To get a sense of how the other brands compare, browse the selection and reviews at: amazon.com or amazon.co.uk.

Various devices, such as this Microsoft Zune, have been touted as "iPod killers", but so far none has made a really significant dent in the iPod's market share.

How do iPods compare to the iPhone?

In 2007 Apple unveiled the iPhone, a bells-and-whistles mobile phone with built-in iPod as well as email and Web access. Apple rightly described the phone as the best iPod they'd ever made.

A few months later came the iPod touch, which is basically the same device without the calling features, the email application (though you can access email via the Web) or the phone-network Internet access (the iPod touch can browse the Web, but only when connected to a Wi-Fi network).

Compared to the iPod classic and nano, the iPhone and iPod touch offer a bigger display, a superior interface and better personal organizer features. But in terms of storage capacity, the iPod classic wins hands down.

For the full story on the iPhone, see this book's sister title, *The Rough Guide to the iPhone*.

Can an iPod hold my whole CD collection?

That depends on the model you buy, the sound quality you desire and – obviously – the size of your collection. The highest-capacity iPod at the time of writing can hold around thirty thousand songs at a sound quality that will satisfy most people: that's enough music to play day and night for more than two months without repeating a single track. So, assuming you own less music than that, you don't insist on super-high fidelity, and you're prepared to pay for a suitably capacious model, then yes, an iPod can hold your whole collection. However, remember that the actual capacity of an iPod is lower than the advertised capacity (see p.30) and if you want to use the iPod for video, photos, podcasts etc, you will be sacrificing potential music-storage space.

It's also worth bearing in mind that in practice you'll need the same amount of space available on the hard drive of your computer, since whatever is on your iPod will typically also live on your PC or Mac...

So I need a computer, too?

Yes – or at the very least you need access to one. A computer is the only way to get a physical music collection onto an iPod. To copy the music from a CD onto an iPod, for example, you first copy it onto the computer (you "rip" it, to use the jargon) and then transfer it from the computer to the Pod. A computer can also be used to download music from the Internet. (You can download tracks directly to an iPod touch over Wi-Fi, but it's fiddly and far easier done using a computer.) More importantly, combining your iPod with a computer ensures that you don't lose all your music and files if your iPod is lost, broken or stolen – you have a complete backup of everything on your Pod.

Is my current computer up to the job?

If you bought a PC or Mac in the last few years, it will probably be capable of working with an iPod, but it's certainly worth checking before blowing all your money. The box overleaf explains the minimum requirements and the upgrade options if your computer doesn't have what it takes.

Computer requirements & upgrade options

Any Mac or PC produced in the last couple of years, including laptops, should be fine for use with an iPod, and many older ones will also work. But it's certainly worth checking your hardware before you buy. The core requirements are a recent operating system and the right socket to plug the iPod into. But you'll also need enough hard drive space to store your music and, ideally, a fast Internet connection. Let's look at these four requirements in turn.

▶ **Windows 7, Vista, XP or 2000, or Mac OS X (v10.4 or later)** To check what operating system you have on a PC, right-click the My Computer icon and select Properties. If you have Windows Me, 98 or 95, you could consider upgrading to XP, Vista or 7, but it will cost you (from $99/£70), it can be a bit of a headache and you'll need to check whether your hardware is up to the job (see *microsoft.com/windows*). Realistically, it's probably also worth considering a new machine. Windows 2000 users should be OK, though you will need to make sure you have downloaded the latest updates from Microsoft via Windows Update in the Start menu.

On a Mac, select About This Mac or System Profiler from the Apple menu. If you have OS X v10.4 or later you'll be OK with any current iPod, though you might have to run the Software Update tool (also in the Apple menu) to grab the latest updates. OS X v10.2 and v10.3 will work with older iPod models only. If you have OS 9 or earlier, then no iPods will work.

Upgrading to the latest version of OS X costs around $130/£90. But first check the minimum requirements to make sure your machine could handle the new operating system (see *apple.com/macosx*).

▶ **USB** This is the computer "port" (socket) to which you connect current iPods. Any USB socket will work, though ideally you want USB2 (found on most PCs and Macs made after 2003), as this makes it more than ten times faster to transfer music and other data to the iPod than old-style USB (check your computer's manual, as USB and USB2 ports look identical).

If you don't have a USB2 port, you could add one to your computer by purchasing a suitable adapter. These are available for as little as $30/£20 for desktops and around double that for laptops. Or, if you have the right port but it's occupied by another device, buy a powered "hub" to turn a single port into two or more. These start at around $30/£20.

Note that many older, full-sized iPods and iPod minis can connect via FireWire (also known by the more prosaic title of IEEE1394) as well as USB.

▶ **Hard drive space** You need enough free hard drive space on your computer to store your digital music and video collections. (It is possible to store the collection just on the iPod, but it's more hassle, less flexible and less secure.)

To find out how big and how full your hard drive is on a PC, open My Computer, right-click the C-drive icon and select Properties. On a Mac, single-click your hard drive icon on the Desktop and select Get Info from the File menu. If you don't have enough space – bearing in mind that you can fit around fifteen to twenty albums on one gigabyte – try deleting any large files that you no longer need (or burning them to CDs) and then empty the Recyle Bin or Trash. On a PC, you could also try running the Disk Cleanup utility: right-click the C-drive icon, select Properties, and then press the Disk Cleanup button.

If you still don't have enough space, consider adding an extra hard drive to your computer: these start at around $50/£30 for one that can be installed inside your computer's body, with higher-capacity and external drives (necessary for laptops) costing more.

▶ **An Internet connection** An Internet connection allows you to do clever things such as automatically add the track details and album artwork for all the music you copy from CD. It also allows you to download music and video from the Internet, subscribe to podcasts and listen to online radio. This is all fine with a broadband connection, but can be frustratingly slow with a dial-up connection.

For everything you need to know about choosing, using and upgrading a PC, Mac or Internet connection, see this book's sister volumes: *The Rough Guide to Windows 7*, *The Rough Guide to Macs & OS X* and *The Rough Guide to the Internet*.

iPods work fine with laptops as well as desktops, and PCs as well as Macs.

What's iTunes?

iTunes is a piece of software, produced by Apple, for importing, downloading, managing and playing music, video and podcasts on a Mac or PC. It's also used for moving audio and video from a computer to an iPod. However, you don't *need* an iPod to use iTunes. If you're mainly interested in creating a music or video collection to enjoy at home – rather than carry around with you – you can do this using iTunes. After all, your computer can do everything an iPod can do, including being hooked up to a hi-fi (see p.177) or television (see p.181).

Another function of iTunes is to provide access to Apple's music, video and app download service – the iTunes Store. You don't have to buy your music from the iTunes Store, of course. You can also use iTunes to play music copied from CD or other computers, or downloaded from elsewhere on the Internet. (However, files from other online stores may not be compatible.)

OK. Sounds good. But...

Isn't it a hassle to transfer all my music from CD to computer to iPod?

It certainly takes a while to transfer a large CD collection onto your computer, but not as long as it would take to play the CDs. Depending on your computer, it can take just a few minutes to transfer the contents of a CD onto your computer's hard drive – and you can listen to the music, or do some work in another application, while this is happening. Still, if you have more money than time, there are services that will take away your CDs and rip them into a well-organized collection for around $1/£1 per CD. See, for example:

PodServe podserve.co.uk (UK)
DMP3 dmp3digital.com (US)
RipDigital ripdigital.com (US)

1. Place your order – we'll help.
2. FedEx your CDs to RipDigital – we supply packing materials and insurance.
3. Receive your digital music library – just plug it in and enjoy.

Once your music is on your PC or Mac, it only takes a matter of minutes to transfer even a large collection across to the iPod; and subsequent transfers from computer to iPod are even quicker, as only new or changed files are copied over.

I've heard the sound quality isn't great.
Is that true?

Audiophiles sometimes turn their noses up at iPods and other digital music players on the grounds that the sound quality is not too
hot. It's true that – at the default settings – the sound is marginally worse than CD, but you're unlikely to notice much, or indeed
any, difference unless you do a careful side-by-side comparison
through a decent home stereo.

  More importantly, this sound quality isn't fixed. When you
import tracks from CD, or record them from other sources, you
can choose from a wide range of options, up to and including full
CD quality. The only problem is that better-quality recordings
take up more disk space, which means fewer tracks on your iPod.
Still, the trade-off between quality and quantity is entirely for you
to decide upon. For more on this, see p.66.

Should I transfer all my DVDs
to my computer too?

No. As we'll see in Chapter 7, it's a bit of a hassle to import DVDs
onto a computer, so it's better to import only those movies which
you want available on your iPod at any one time. In addition, be
aware that each DVD you import will require plenty of free disk
space on your computer and iPod.

How's the video quality?

It goes without saying that an iPod screen can't compare with
that of a television set. That said, the quality is higher than you
might expect, since the iPod packs more pixels into each square
inch of screen than a regular television. Videos downloaded from
the iTunes store will generally look slightly better than those you

import from DVD, which can look pixelated, especially in dark, shadowy sequences with subtle variations in hue.

Aside from the iPod, iTunes makes a good tool for managing video files on a Mac or PC; you can use it to play them back via either the computer screen or a connected television (see p.181).

What if my computer dies?

Hard drives occasionally give up the ghost, in which case the only chance of getting any of the contents back is a time-consuming and potentially expensive data-recovery process. And, of course, computers meet many other nasty ends: theft, lightning, spilled coffee and so on. If this happens, and you lose all the music and video stored on the hard drive, it can be a real pain.

However, with a little know-how (see p.236) it's possible to move all your files back from your iPod onto a new hard drive or computer. (Apple tend to keep this relatively quiet, since it makes it very easy to illegally distribute your music collection onto your friends' computers.) Obviously, you'll only be able to transfer what's on the iPod at that time, so if you don't keep your entire collection on both your computer and your iPod, it's definitely worth backing up your computer's hard drive (see p.245).

What was the furore in the press about iPod batteries?

The current generation of iPods have rechargeable, lithium-ion batteries, much like the ones in laptop computers. After a full charge, which takes between two and four hours, these can provide enough power to play up to thirty-six hours of music (depending on the model) and/or remain on standby for days. However, like all such batteries, they don't live forever. After five hundred or so full recharges – which could be anywhere between two and ten years' usage – they start holding less and less power before eventually dying completely.

When iPod users first realized this, they were shocked to learn that the battery was not user-replaceable and that to have it replaced by Apple would cost so much that they might as well bin the iPod and buy a new one. After much public pressure

The Neistat Brothers were so upset when they realized their iPod batteries were effectively non-replaceable, they felt compelled to make a film. Happily, the batteries can now be replaced for much less than the price of a new iPod.

and a few legal threats, however, Apple dropped the price of the service to $99 in the US, and an equivalent amount elsewhere (still a lot, though no more than an average laptop battery). Since then, various third-party services have popped up offering a much cheaper "unofficial" service. If you look online, you'll also find batteries for sale, with instructions for doing it yourself. For more info, see p.255.

Isn't this whole thing just another consumerist fad from a money-grabbing music industry?

The extraordinary range of music formats we've had in the last half-century – vinyl, cassette, CD, DAT, MiniDisc, SACD – has often been described as a cynical ploy by the music and electronics industries to make us buy ever more equipment and multiple copies of the same recordings. Whatever your view on this, digital music players such as the iPod are qualitatively different from the rest. For a start, they certainly weren't dreamed up by the music industry: in fact, the music industry is quaking in its boots about anything that combines music with computers, since the world of "digital music" makes it incredibly easy to illegally share copyrighted material – both via the Internet or simply by copying, say, five hundred albums from a friend's computer in minutes.

As for whether iPods are another unnecessary consumer fad from the electronics industry, this is a matter for debate. True, they're ultimately expensive gadgets bought by the relatively wealthy and manufactured in an oppressive regime where labour rights tend to be poor (China). The same is true for much electronic equipment. But from an environmental perspective, you can make at least some defence for a device that deals with music purely as digital data: downloading, compared to buying CDs, means no more delivery trucks and no more unnecessary packaging. An iPod, after all, only weighs as much as a single boxed CD, but can hold the same amount of music as several thousand.

Is copying and downloading music illegal?

No. The only thing that's illegal is taking copyrighted material that you haven't acquired legitimately – and, of course, distributing copyrighted material that you have acquired legitimately. You're well within your rights to copy your own music collection onto your computer and iPod, as long as you don't then copy the files onto your friends' computers or iPods. As for music on the Internet, there are numerous legal options, including online services that sell individual tracks to download and keep, and others which offer unlimited access to a music archive in return for a monthly fee. There's also plenty of downloadable music that's both legal and free: one-off promotions from major labels, for example, and songs by little-known musicians more interested in establishing their name than making a profit.

However, it's true that, at present, much copyrighted material is downloaded from file-sharing networks such as KaZaA (see p.112). Though you are unlikely to get prosecuted for taking part in this free-for-all, it is definitely illegal. For the full lowdown on downloading, see chapters 9 and 10.

What's DRM?

As we've already seen, there's nothing the record industry fears more – understandably enough – than the uncontrolled distribution of its copyrighted music. It's hard to see how the record companies will ever be able to stop people sharing files they have copied from their own CDs, even if they succeed in killing off file-sharing networks like KaZaA.

One strategy that both labels and online music retailers have employed for stopping people freely distributing tracks they've purchased and downloaded from legitimate online music stores is called DRM – digital rights management. It involves embedding special code into music files (or other formats, such as movie files) to impose certain restrictions on what you can do with them – for example, stopping you from burning files to CD, or transferring them to an iPod.

Is that an infringement of my rights?

This is a hotly debated issue. Advocates of the free distribution of music see DRM as an infringement of their rights, while others see it as a legitimate way for record labels and retailers to safeguard their products from piracy.

However, the DRM debate is really just one part of a bigger argu-

As this poster available from *modernhumorist. com* shows, many on the "free distribution" side of the DRM debate see their adversaries – led by the Recording Industry Association of America – as draconian authoritarians committed only to profit, power, and an outmoded and unsustainable business model. Unsurprisingly, many musicians disagree.

ment about whether it's ethical to "share" copyrighted music – and other so-called intellectual property. The sharers claim that music is about art not money; that most of the artists whose tracks are being downloaded are already millionaires; that sharing is a great way to experience new music (some of which you might then buy on CD); and that if the record industry really is in trouble, they deserve it for ripping off consumers with overpriced albums for so many years. The industry, on the other hand, says that sharing – or theft, as they prefer to put it – deprives artists of royalties and record labels of the money they need to invest in future albums. The result, they claim, will be fewer musicians and less new music.

Where does iTunes stand on the use of DRM?

Historically, music downloaded from the iTunes Store was embedded with DRM which stopped you from making the tracks available on more than a certain number of computers at one time or copying it to non-iPod MP3 players. In January 2009, however, Apple announced that all music sold through the store would be completely DRM-free within a matter of months. Though video files and apps downloaded from the Store *do* still contain DRM that prevents their free distribution, the move by Apple to make iTunes Store music DRM-free has been seen by many as a final nail in the coffin of this approach to copyright protection.

While many iTunes consumers are more than happy with the final result, there remains a complex debate. The arguments encompass the very concept of intellectual property, the different views on the effect of downloading on CD sales, and even touch upon completely new models for reimbursing musicians – such as the Internet-based "music tax" advocated by some experts. For both sides of the debate, see:

Recording Industry Association of America riaa.com
Electronic Frontier Foundation eff.org
The Register theregister.com/music_media

What about all my CDs?

Unless you're a sound-quality connoisseur or a fan of sleeve notes, you might find that once your music collection has been copied onto your computer and iPod, the original CDs start to seem like a waste of space. Some people have advocated selling them: after all, many CDs will go for $10/£5 on eBay, so if you sell enough you could end up far better off than before you bought your iPod. Strictly speaking, though, this is legally dodgy: the moment you sell the CD you are no longer the rightful owner of the music, and technically you should remove the tracks from your computer and Pod.

Getting technical

How is the music stored?

Clever though computers are, they only deal in numbers – digital, rather than analogue, information. In fact, their vocabulary is limited to just zeros and ones: the "binary" number system. So music on a computer or iPod – whether it's a folk song or a symphony – is reduced to a series of millions of zeros or ones. Or, more accurately, it's reduced to a series of tiny magnetic or electronic charges, each representing a zero or a one. A typical song would consist of around 30 million zeros and ones, while an 80GB hard drive in an iPod or computer can hold around 600 billion zeros and ones – roughly 100 for every person on the planet.

But aren't CDs also "digital"?

Absolutely. The idea of reducing music to zeros and ones is nothing new: CDs, MiniDiscs and any other "digital" formats also store music as zeros and ones. But none of these other formats combines the capacity, flexibility and editability of an iPod.

What exactly is an MP3?

Computers store information – such as spreadsheets and images – as "files", and there are various different formats for each kind of file. A fancy text document created in Microsoft Word, for example, is saved in the "doc" format, while a simpler text-only document with no styling is usually saved as a "txt" file. Likewise, a professional-quality photo might be a "tif", while the same image displayed on a website would probably be a JPEG, which looks very nearly as good but is incomparably quicker to download. The format is usually included in a file's name – John.jpg, for example.

Music on computers (and iPods) can be stored in numerous file formats, but the main ones you need to know about are the ubiquitous MP3 (or Moving Pictures Experts Group-1/2 Audio Layer 3 to give it its rather grandiose full title) and the more recent AAC (Advanced Audio Coding).

Like JPEGs for images, these music formats are designed for squeezing lots of information into very small files; in fact, technically speaking, the names MP3 and AAC refer not just to the file format but also to the "compression algorithms" used to do the squeezing. Each format has its pros and cons (see p.65), but they both achieve pretty amazing feats of compression. When a computer turns the uncompressed audio information on a CD into MP3 or AAC, the resulting file sounds almost identical to the original but is around ninety percent smaller. That means ten times as much music on your iPod and ten times quicker downloads from the Internet.

This compression is achieved through a remarkable combination of mathematics and psychoacoustics: the algorithms are clever enough to take out what your brain does not process (the vast majority of the sound) and leave the rest untouched. For a full explanation, see mp3-converter.com/mp3codec.

Amazing. But my vinyl junkie friends tell me that CDs are also compressed. Is that true?

Technically speaking, yes, any digital recording could be described as being compressed, since taking the infinitely rich and varied analogue sounds of the real world and turning them into a finite series of numbers inevitably involves losing something. Indeed, many people prefer vinyl (which isn't digital) to CDs for just this reason: they claim it sounds richer and more real. But that's a separate discussion. The point here is that, in the context of iPods, MP3s and the like, "compression" refers to the compressing of digital files into smaller digital files, not the compression of the music into numbers.

Each individual track can be compressed to a greater or lesser extent. This is measured in terms of bitrates.

What's a bitrate?

The bitrate of a digital music file is the amount of data (the number of "bits", or zeros and ones) that is used to encode each second of music. This is measured in kbps: kilo (thousand) bits per second. (Incidentally, if you've ever heard of a "56k modem", the k in that context is short for kbps and means exactly the same thing: the number of bits transferred per second.)

Most music files are encoded at a bitrate of 128, 160 or 192kbps, which means that each second of sound is made up of around 100,000 to 200,000 zeros and ones. However, higher and lower bitrates are not uncommon, the latter often being used for spoken-word recordings, where the sound quality is not quite so important.

How big is a gig?

The storage capacity of iPods, like other hard drives, is measured in gigabytes – also known as gigs or GBs. Roughly speaking, a byte is eight zeros and ones (the space required on a computer disk to store a single character of text), and a gigabyte is a billion bytes. To compare to other file sizes that you may have come across, a gig is the same as 1000MB (megabytes) or 1,000,000KB (kilobytes).

Mathematically minded readers may be interested to know that all these figures are actually approximations of the number two raised to different powers. A gigabyte is two bytes to the power of thirty, which equals 1,073,741,824 bytes. To find out what you can actually squeeze into a gig, turn to p.31.

And finally...

Anything else I should know?

In brief, a few common confounders expounded:

►**You can't copy music from an iPod to a computer** At least not without extra software (see p.236). The standard setup is that your iPod simply mirrors the Library on your computer.

►**You can't delete music from an iPod directly** You have to do it via iTunes. See p.58.

► **Playlists are *not* folders containing music files** A playlist is simply a list of songs – adding a song to more than one playlist doesn't duplicate the file, and deleting a playlist doesn't delete the songs in it.

►**You don't need to type in CD track names manually** Almost invariably, someone has already done it for you. See p.62.

► **Not all iPods fit the same docks** Always make sure that the Dock adapter you are using (on both Apple and third-party equipment) is right for your model of iPod (see p.39). Trying to force an iPod into a Dock adapter that's too small is futile, while balancing a Pod in an adapter that's too big is likely to damage the connector.

02

Buying an iPod

Which model? Where from?

There have been various iPod models over the years, but at the time of going to press there are only four types in production: the iPod classic, the iPod nano, the iPod shuffle and the iPod touch. All except the shuffle can handle video and photos and connect to a TV to play them back. When buying an iPod it's worth being aware of all the specific features of each model, and not simply judging your decision based upon price, capacity or … colour. That said, you have to start somewhere: if you want added functionality look seriously at the touch *and* the apps available for it; if you have a large music collection, investigate the iPod classic; and if you are looking to coordinate an outfit, you are probably going to kick off by looking at the nanos. Here's a little more on each iPod in turn:

iPod touch

The touch features a huge display and a touch-screen interface – just like the iPhone. It can be used in both portrait and landscape orientations thanks to its nifty accelerometer (a device that basically tells the iPod which way around it is being held, allowing you to control the device by tilting and shaking it). The touch also offers access to the Web, email and iTunes Store via Wi-Fi, and provides decent PDA features. Its functionality is almost limitless thanks to downloadable apps (see p.119), many of which are free. It has a built-in speaker, and is currently available in three storage sizes, each with an attractive mirrored backside.

▶ **Screen** 3.5-inch (diagonal), Multi-Touch, colour, widescreen.

▶ **Capacity** 1750 (8GB model), 3500 (16GB model) or 7000 (32GB model) songs*.

▶ **Battery life** Up to 36 hrs of music playback; 6 hrs of video playback.

*Capacity calculations based upon 4-minute songs encoded as 128kbps AAC files.

iPod classic

The iPod classic has been around since September 2007, when it replaced the fifth-generation iPod (also known as the "video iPod"). The classic comes in either black or brushed-aluminium, though its primary attraction is its massive storage capacity.

▶ **Screen** 2.5-inch (diagonal), colour.

▶ **Capacity** 30,000 (120GB model) songs*.

▶ **Battery life** Up to 36 hrs of music playback; 6 hrs of video playback.

Phones as iPods

Futurologists have for many years talked about "convergence" – the idea that multiple devices will gradually be replaced by newer devices capable of fulfilling more than one function. One obvious example is the gradual combination of MP3 players and mobile phones.

Many mobiles can play music, but until 2007 the only ones compatible with iTunes were a few models by Motorola – an Apple partnership spawned in 2005 with the launch of the ROKR EI handset. These phones, however, only hold a relatively small number of songs, and their interface left rather a lot to be desired.

All this changed with the appearance of the iPhone (see p.8), which at the time of its launch was described by Apple as "the best iPod we've ever made".

*Capacity calculations based upon 4-minute songs encoded as 128kbps AAC files.

iPod nano

Now in their fourth generation, nanos have a much smaller capacity than the classic (with a choice of either 8GB or 16GB models). They come in a variety of colours (a range that Apple marketeers have dubbed "nano-chromatic") and like the touch, have an accelerometer that lets you shake the iPod to shuffle playback; it also switches the display to Cover Flow mode (see p.130) when the iPod is held sideways. Like the iPod shuffle and iPod touch, the nano stores data on internal flash memory rather than a hard drive, which makes it less prone to skipping and likely to prove more durable than the iPod classic.

▶ **Screen** 2-inch (diagonal), colour, widescreen.

▶ **Capacity** 2000 (8GB model) or 4000 (16GB model) songs*.

▶ **Battery life** Up to 36 hrs of music playback; 6 hrs of video playback.

*Capacity calculations based upon 4-minute songs encoded as 128kbps AAC files.

iPod shuffle

The smallest (at only 45mm long) and least expensive member of the iPod family is eminently portable but lacks a screen and so doesn't allow any visual browsing of the music stored on it. That said, it can be set to announce the titles of artists, songs and playlists with a feature called VoiceOver (see p.57). The current iPod shuffle can hold around 1000 songs at any one time, and also handle multiple playlist (where its predecessors could manage only one). It is available in either black or brushed-aluminium and both charges and syncs via a special USB cable that plugs into the device's headphone socket. Contrary to popular misconception, you can play through the playlist not only randomly (in "shuffle" mode) but also in fixed order. One drawback of the iPod shuffle, however, is that the player's controls are located half way along the cord of the bundled Apple earphones, making it impossible to use an alternative set of headphones without shelling out for a third-party controller or adapter. For more on using an iPod shuffle, see p.47.

▶ **Screen** None.

▶ **Capacity** 1000 (4GB model) songs*.

▶ **Battery life** Up to 10 hrs of music playback.

*Capacity calculations based upon 4-minute songs encoded as 128kbps AAC files.

How many gigs do you need?

Choosing between the various iPod models is partly a matter of choosing how much storage capacity to go for. Remember that you don't necessarily need an iPod capable of holding your whole music or video collection – or even the collection you intend to digitize. You can store your whole collection on your computer's hard drive and just copy across to your iPod the songs or albums you want to listen to at any one time.

Also worth bearing in mind when it comes to storage capacity is that if you plan to use the iPod as a portable hard drive (see p.189), as well as a digital media player, you'll need enough extra space available for the kinds of files you're

True storage capacity

All computer storage devices are in reality about seven percent smaller than advertised. The reason for this is that hardware manufacturers use gigabyte to mean one billion bytes, whereas in computing reality it should be 1.0737 billion bytes. This is a bit of a scam, but everyone does it and no one wants to break the mould. So an 8GB iPod nano is really only around 7.5 gigs. What's more, some of the capacity is also taken up by the firmware that makes the iPod work.

To view the real capacity of your iPod, connect it to your computer and look under the Summary tab of the iPod Options panel in iTunes. The figure is displayed to the left of the colourful iPod capacity meter.

planning on storing. Word and Excel docs and the like are almost negligibly small, but backing up your whole system or storing image, video or program files quickly fills up space. Finally, note that the actual formatted capacity of an iPod – like all computer storage devices – is slightly smaller than what's advertised (see box opposite).

Checking your current data needs

If you already use iTunes to store music and video, then you can easily get an idea of how much space your existing collection takes up. On the left, click Music, Movies, Podcasts or any playlist and the bottom of the iTunes window will reveal the total disk space that the selected item occupies.

As for photographs, the size of the images on your computer and the amount of space they occupy there bears little relation to the space the same images would take up on an iPod. This is because when iTunes copies photos to your Pod, it re-sizes them for use on that model's screen. As a rough guide, three thousand images will take up around 1GB on your iPod.

What can you fit in a gigabyte?		
	Audio Quality	**1GB =**
Music	at 128kbps (normal quality)	250 typical tracks
	at 256kbps (high quality)	125 typical tracks
	at 992kbps (CD quality)	32 typical tracks
Audiobooks	at 32kbps	70 hours
Photos	–	3000 photos
Video	–	2.5 hours

Where to buy

As with all Apple products, iPods cost basically the same amount no matter where you buy them. The price you'll get direct from Apple…

Apple Store UK apple.com/ukstore ► 0800/039-1010
Apple Store US apple.com/store ► 1-800/MY-APPLE

…will typically be only a few pounds/dollars more (or occasionally less) than the price you'll find from the many other dealers that sell online or on the high street. That said, different sellers may throw in different extras, from engraving on the back of the iPod to a pair of portable speakers. In the US market you can keep track of these various offers and discounts at the brilliant "Buyers' Guides" section of:

Mac Review Zone macreviewzone.com

Or try a price-comparison agent such as, in the US:

Google Product Search google.com/products
PriceWatch pricewatch.com
Shopper.com shopper.com
Shopping.com shopping.com

In the UK, price-comparison agents include:

Kelkoo kelkoo.co.uk
Shopping.com uk.shopping.com

Buying from a "real" high-street store typically means paying the full standard price, but you'll get the iPod immediately. If you order over the phone or Internet from Apple, you can expect up to a week's wait for delivery. For a list of dealers in the UK, follow the link from apple.com/uk/hardware.

> **TIP:** You can get ten percent off the retail price of any iPod at the Apple Store if you trade in an old iPod to be recycled. Currently this offer is only available in the US.

In many US and UK cities, you can also go straight to one of Apple's own high-street stores, such as the New York City branch pictured below. For a list of all the stores, see:

Apple Stores apple.com/retail

However, some online retailers tend to be quite quick to deliver, including the best known of all:

Amazon US amazon.com
Amazon UK amazon.co.uk

Used iPods

Refurbished iPods

Apple, and a few retailers, offer refurbished iPods. These are either end-of-line models or up-to-date ones which have been returned for some reason. They come "as new" – checked, repackaged and with a full standard warranty – but they are reduced in price by up to 40 percent (usually more like 15 percent). The only problem is availability: the products are in such hot demand that you need to check in regularly to see the real bargains, and when you do see something you want, don't think you have that much time to mull over the purchase, as it will probably go to someone else if you decide to sleep on it.

In both the UK and US sites, follow the Special Deals links from apple.com/ukstore and apple.com/store respectively; and in the US, for the most up-to-date information about availability, call 1-800/MY-APPLE. Alternatively, check with your local Apple retailer to see whether they offer refurbished or returned iPods.

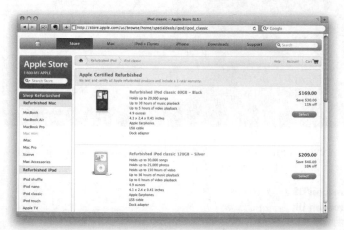

Secondhand iPods

Buying a secondhand iPod is much like buying any other piece of used electronic equipment: you might find a bargain but you might land yourself with an overpriced bookend. If you buy one that is less than a year old, it will still be within warranty, so you should be able to get it repaired for free if anything goes wrong inside – even if the iPod in question was purchased in a different country.

Whatever you buy, it's good to see it in action before parting with any cash, but remember that this won't tell you everything. If an iPod's been used a lot, for example, the battery might be on its last legs and soon need replacing, which will add substantially to the cost (see p.255). Also remember that older models won't necessarily support more recent accessories or software.

If you buy on eBay, you'll get loads of choice and a certain level of protection against getting sold a dud. But be sure to read the auction listing carefully and ask the seller questions if you're unsure of anything.

Laser engraving

If you purchase from Apple, you'll be offered the chance to have a name, slogan or whatever typographic message you like laser-engraved on the iPod's shiny backside. This is the iPod equivalent of a tattoo, so think very carefully, as you're stuck with it. If you want a few ideas, or just to laugh at some of the best and worst engravings ever requested, visit:

Technology Madness technologymadness.com/?p=217
Methodshop methodshop.com/gadgets/humor/rejectedengraving

Security-conscious iPod buyers could consider getting their name and either an email address or telephone number engraved on their new gadget. This will give it at least a fighting chance of finding its way back to you if lost; and, if stolen, the thief will have a hard time selling it on.

iPod hard drive upgrades

If you have an older iPod that you are looking to replace because it no longer has the capacity that you need, it's worth knowing that there are companies out there that can upgrade the hard drives of many older iPod models for something far more capacious. US firm RapidRepair, for example, can squeeze a 240GB drive into an old iPod Video. It's not cheap, and will most likely void your Apple warranty, but what you get is double the drive space of the roomiest iPod currently available from Apple.

RapidRepair rapidrepair.com

To buy or to wait?

When shopping for any piece of computer equipment, there's always the tricky question of whether to buy the current model, which may have been around for a few months, or hang on for the next version, which may be better *and* less expensive. In the case of iPods, the situation is worse than normal, because Apple are famously secretive about their plans to release new or upgraded versions of their hardware.

Unless you have a friend who works in Apple HQ – and an opportunity to get them drunk – you're unlikely to hear anything from the horse's mouth about new iPod models until the day they appear. So, unless a new model came out recently, there's always the possibility that your new purchase will be out of date within a few weeks. About the best you can do is check out some sites where rumours of new models are discussed. But don't believe everything you read…

Apple Insider appleinsider.com
Mac Rumors macrumors.com
Think Secret thinksecret.com

03

Getting started

Installing, filling and using an iPod

S etting up iTunes and an iPod on your computer isn't difficult, but it pays to take a few moments to understand the various setup options and controls, and the different ways that an iPod can sync with iTunes.

Plugging in, charging up

Cables

Each of the currently available iPods comes with a USB2 cable, which will connect to your computer or, if you have one, an AC power adapter. Back in the day, iPods came with FireWire cables, but these have gradually been phased out, and the current members of the iPod family can only talk to iTunes via USB2.

The flat connector slots into your iPod or Dock. Some older iPod cable connectors have almost invisible release buttons on their sides which need to be gently squeezed when disconnecting. Newer models (pictured) don't, but simply come loose with a gentle, even tug. Never force a connector as you risk damaging either the connector or socket.

Extra iPod cables by Apple and various third parties are widely available. It you use your iPod as a hard drive, it can be handy to have two – one at home, the other in your bag or briefcase.

> **TIP:** iPod and iPhone cables are interchangeable. You can also swap Docks between iPods and iPhones, though only the iPhone Dock features holes allowing the phone's speaker and mic to be accessible while Docked.

Docks

A dock is a small stand that provides a secure spot for your iPod and makes it easy for you to connect to a computer, power socket or hi-fi (see p.177). All iPods except the shuffle (which comes bundled with its own special cable as it's really to small to use with a dock) ship with a dock adapter – a piece of molded plastic for that specific model which can then be slotted into an Apple Universal Dock (see p.228).

Various other companies produce iPod docks that work with multiple iPod models, though it is always worth checking that your Pod is supported before you buy.

iPod charging

To charge an iPod, simply connect it to the USB port on a computer or power adapter. Note, however, that if you're charging via a computer, the USB port in question will need to be "powered". The vast majority of USB sockets meet this criterion, but some, especially those on keyboards and other peripherals, may not work. Also note that your iPod usually won't charge from a Mac or PC in sleep or standby mode.

Like many similar devices, iPods use a combination of "fast" and "trickle" charging. This means that, with an iPod classic for example, it should take around two hours to achieve an eighty percent charge, and another two hours to get to one hundred percent. A new, fully charged iPod should provide between ten and thirty-six hours of music playback (see pp.26–29), though just leaving the device lying around and not playing will cause the power level to drain gradually. As the battery ages, expect the maximum playback time to reduce. For tips on maximizing your battery life, see p.254.

If you are unable to charge your Pod via your computer, or you want to be able to charge when away from home, consider buying a separate power adapter. Available from Apple, these cost $29/£19 – much to the annoyance of many iPod owners, as they shipped as standard with earlier models.

When an iPod with a hard drive (such as a classic or any older full-size iPod) is plugged into your computer, its drive will stay active, which some users see as unnecessary wear and tear. If this thought bothers you, consider "ejecting" the Pod (see p.48); this puts it into charge-only mode and puts the drive in standby mode.

Installing

If you already use iTunes

If iTunes is already installed on your computer – as is the case for all recent Macs – you may find you can simply connect your iPod and everything will work just fine. However, you may first need to update your copy of iTunes (see below).

If you don't already use iTunes

If you have a PC and you've never used iTunes, you'll need to install it. Get online and go straight to apple.com/itunes to download the most up-to-date version.

Once downloaded, simply double-click the installer file and follow the prompts. At some stage, you'll be invited to choose a name for your new Pod, which is no laughing matter (see box opposite), and select from a few simple installation options. Unless you have a reason not to, stick with the default choices.

Grab the latest version

It's always worth using the most recent version of iTunes to make sure your system is stable, secure and offers all the latest features. From time to time, you may be prompted to update iTunes automatically, but you can also do it manually. On a Mac, click Apple menu > Software Update and any new versions will appear in the list. On a PC, open iTunes and hit Help > Check For iTunes Updates.

To make sure that your iPod is running the latest version of its internal software, connect it to your computer, click its icon in iTunes and click the Check For Update button.

The name game

Judging by the number of online chat forums devoted to the subject, naming an iPod is a serious business. The obvious move is to call it "John's Pod", "Jane's Pod", or whatever, but we think you can do better than that. Here are a few weird and wonderful ideas plucked from the World Wide Web:

"I was thinking and thinking of a name for my mini … I looked up Greek and Latin roots and named it 'Parfichlorolocuphone', which means small, green, sound speaker…"
GreenerMini

"doPi (ipod backward) the music elf, as in harry potter rip off of dobby the house elf…"
tombo_jombo

"My iPod's name is 'Glitch', because I had to set it up with Win98SE…"
jesspark

For more inspiration, search Google Groups (*google.com/groups*), or search "Does your iPod have a name" in the forums section of ilounge (*ilounge.com/forums*). If you've already named your iPod, it's not too late to change it: just double-click its name in the iTunes Sources sidebar and type something else. But be sure to bear in mind this essential advice…

"Its [sic] not bad to change the iPod's name as long as you sit down with it and have a long conversation about what it thinks is best for it."
Kurt8374

iTunes at a glance

Volume slider Only applies to iTunes; the maximum volume is defined by your computer's master volume control.

Main play controls Others can be found in the Controls menu, via the keyboard (see the inside back cover of this book) and, on a Mac, by clicking and holding on the iTunes icon in The Dock.

Divider Drag here to change the size of the Sources sidebar.

Sources sidebar Situated on the left, the Sources sidebar is the doorway to your music and video collection, various radio stations (see p.117), other people's shared music (see p.185) and the iTunes Store (see p.97). It also lists attached devices such as iPods, CDs and Apple TVs (see p.182).

Add a playlist See p.140 for more info.

Shuffle Play currently displayed tracks in random order.

Repeat Click once to repeat all songs currently displayed, twice to repeat just one song.

Open artwork panel See p.156 for more on album artwork.

Status area Displays info about the track currently playing or importing and, when you click the small triangular icon on its left, becomes an attractive but fairly worthless EQ display.

View options Lets you chose between List view, Grid view and Cover Flow view. See pp.126–130.

Search Enter one or more words or partial words or search whatever songs or videos are currently displayed in the main panel.

Column headers Click a header to sort songs by that column, or drag the columns left and right to reposition. For more information, see p.126.

Main panel Displays the songs or videos for whatever you have selected in the Sources sidebar.

Genius Controls The first of these two buttons either starts or refreshes the Genius playlist (see p.134); the second button opens and closes the Genius Sidebar.

Info Tells you the total length and file size of all the songs or videos currently displayed. Click once for a more accurate version.

Remote speakers Lists any attached AirPort Express units on your home network. See p.178 for more information.

Syncing: filling your iPod

To fill up your iPod, you first need to create a collection of music, video and podcasts in iTunes, as described in the following chapters. Then you simply connect your iPod and choose which of these items you'd like to copy over.

This is done using the iPod Options panel which is accessed by clicking your iPod's icon within iTunes (pictured below). The tabs at the top of the panel provide access to the settings for music, photos, video and so on. Have a look through and see how you'd like everything to work.

For each category you can either upload everything to your iPod or be selective and choose specific playlists (for music and video), albums (for photos), groups (for contacts) and so on. With an iPod touch, you can also copy across your Web bookmarks. When you are done, hit Apply, then Sync.

Click the iPod icon to reveal the Summary and sync screens.

Explore the tabs to control what is copied to your iPod.

The capacity meter at the bottom of the Summary area shows you how much space each type of media is taking up, and how much space you have left.

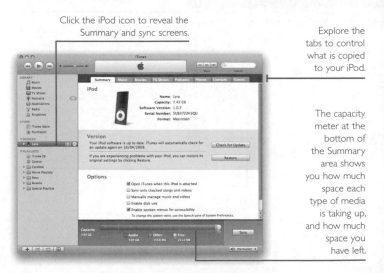

The option of uploading specific playlists can be very useful if you have an iPod without the capacity to hold your whole collection; if you want to save time when updating your iPod; or if you want to leave some space on your Pod for non-music files. It's also handy if you're using multiple iPods with a single iTunes library – each user can simply organize their preferred tracks into a specific set of playlists. For more on playlists, see p.139.

> **TIP:** If you use your iPod as a hard drive (see p.189) and move files to the Trash to make more space available, the reclaimed space will not register on the iTunes iPod meter, or be available to use, until you empty your computer's Trash.

Automatic vs manual syncing

By default, the iPod operates by so-called automatic syncing. That means it simply reflects all or part of the collection stored on your computer. If you delete something from your computer, it will be deleted from your iPod next time you sync. Likewise if you add something, or change a track name, and so on.

Automatic syncing is the most convenient option for most circumstances, but if you prefer you can manage your music and video manually. This option – enabled by checking the box under the Summary tab – gives you complete control over the contents of your iPod. When selected, you simply drag tracks, albums, artists, playlists, genres or movies from your iTunes collection onto

> **TIP:** If your iPod is set to update automatically and you want to stop this from happening (for example, to access iPod Preferences and turn off automatic updating) hold down ⌘~ (on a Mac) or Ctrl-Alt (on a PC) for a few seconds while attaching the iPod.

the iPod's icon (as pictured). You can also drag directly into any playlists on the iPod – click the small triangle next to the iPod's icon in the Sources sidebar to view them.

In this manual mode you can also remove songs or playlists from your iPod. Click the triangle next to the Pod's icon and browse; select one or more items in the main iTunes panel and then select Clear from the Edit menu. Note that removing a song from a playlist only removes it from the playlist – not from the actual iPod.

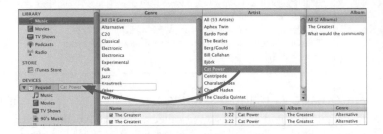

Adding content from other computers

If you're using the default, automatic syncing setup, when you plug your iPod into someone else's computer iTunes will offer to completely replace your media with theirs. (Unless, that is, you're connecting a Mac-formatted iPod to a PC, in which case it won't work at all: see p.91.) If you say yes, next time you connect at home you'll get the same choice – keep the new content or replace it with your own.

This setup is designed to prevent the unauthorized copying of music. However, it's a real pain if you have more than one computer, or if you want to copy something copyright-free from a friend's Mac or PC.

To get around this, you could switch to manual syncing, as described above. This way you can connect your iPod to as many computers as you like and copy tracks and videos from each.

However, if you ever switch back to automatic mode, everything will be removed from the Pod to be replaced by the collection from whichever PC or Mac you're going to sync with.

For this reason, a better alternative is to enable your iPod as a hard drive and use it to transfer the actual song files from one computer to the other. To find out how, see Chapter 8.

TIP: When a manually managed iPod is connected, iTunes lets you browse and play its contents. Click the triangle next to the iPod's icon to get started. A handy way to play your music at a friend's house.

Filling up an iPod shuffle

The screenless iPod shuffle works similarly to its bigger cousins, though its iTunes Options panel only offers tabs for Summary, Music and Podcasts.

There are two options for filling a shuffle with music. You can have iTunes add tracks randomly from either a specific playlist or your entire collection using the Autofill option under the Music tab, or, select the Manually manage music option under the Summary tab and then drag individual songs and playlists onto the Pod. If you manage music yourself, you must eject the iPod shuffle (see p.48) from the iTunes Sources sidebar before you can disconnect it.

The space available for music depends on whether you select Enable disk use under the Summary tab. If you do, you can choose how much space to dedicate to music and how much to dedicate to data.

Note that the iPod shuffle won't play space-heavy Apple Lossless files, or any files with a bitrate higher than 320kbps. However, this isn't a problem as, under Summary, you'll find an option to have iTunes automatically convert higher-quality files to 128kbps on the fly. Nearby, you'll also see an option for enabling the spoken VoiceOver browsing feature (see p.57 for more on this) and the language you want it to natter in. You can also set the language used for specific tracks by highlighting them in iTunes and selecting File > Get Info; then look for the dropdown under the Options tab. This can be useful for foreign tracks and some classical pieces that, say, you want VoiceOver to recognize as being Italian.

Back in the shuffle's Summary panel, check that everything is set just the way you want it, hit Apply, then Sync.

Disconnecting an iPod

Depending on a few factors, an attached iPod may display the warning "Do not disconnect" on its screen. If so, you'll need to "eject" your iPod before unplugging the cable. To do this, either:

⏶ **Click the eject icon** to the right of the iPod icon (pictured) in the Sources sidebar.

⏶ **Right-click the iPod icon** in the Sources sidebar and select Eject…

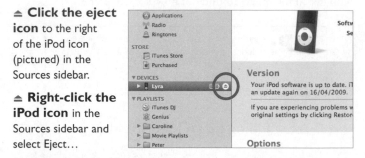

⏶ **Click the Controls menu** at the top of iTunes and select the Eject "iPod's name" option.

⏶ **Use your keyboard** On a PC hit Ctrl+E and on a Mac use ⌘E.

⏶ **Drag your iPod's Desktop icon to the Trash** (only works on Macs, and with Disk Use enabled; see p.190).

If you simply disconnect the device without properly dismounting it, you could end up mashing song data, crashing your computer or even damaging the hard drive in your iPod, so get into the habit of doing it properly. And even when following one of the correct procedures, don't physically pull the plug, or remove your Pod from the Dock, until the iPod's screen displays the regular menu. On older Pods a large tick icon appears to inform you that the dismount was successful.

If the iPod refuses to unmount, and the "Do not disconnect" message stays on the screen, there may be a problem. Turn to the Help! chapter (see p.250).

Using a click-wheel iPod

The iPod controls have altered slightly with each new design, but whichever you have, they're pretty intuitive.

Browsing and playing

The diagram overleaf shows what each button does on a click-wheel iPod – that is, an iPod with buttons integrated at four compass points of a scroll wheel. Besides the controls mentioned here, there are also button combinations used for troubleshooting and resetting (see p.251).

The iPod's hierarchy of menus and sub-menus is largely self-explanatory and best explored by trial and error, so we won't bore you with a step-by-step guide. Suffice to say that you browse menus by moving a thumb or finger around the click wheel and click the central button to select something. If you find yourself lost, simply backtrack using the Menu button until you know where you are again.

Shuffle and Repeat on the iPod

The main menu on recent iPods contains an option to Shuffle Songs, which picks tracks randomly from your entire collection. If you look within the Settings menu, however, you'll find more advanced options. If you turn on Shuffle here, individual playlists or albums will play back in random order. And you can also opt to Shuffle by albums instead of tracks. The same menu also gives you options for Repeat, but bear in mind that if your iPod is set to play forever, you'll be more likely to run down your battery (or damage your earphones) if you forget to use the Hold switch and the Pod gets turned on accidentally in your pocket.

The Shuffle option can also be changed when you are listening to music and viewing the Now Playing screen; simple click the Select button either three times (classic) or four times (nano) to reveal the toggle switch.

Click-wheel iPods at a glance

Hold switch Get used to using this to disable the other controls – especially when you're not using your iPod.

Select button Use this to make selections in menus, or start playing a highlighted song. When a tune is playing, the button also selects between volume, rating, Genius and scrubbing. Held down it displays a menu of other options; on older click-wheel models this toggles the backlight on and off.

MENU As well as taking you back through the menus when clicked, this button turns on the iPod's backlight when held down.

Click wheel Besides letting you scroll through menus, this wheel alters the volume when you're listening to music. It also features the four main control buttons.

I◄◄ One click takes you back to the start of a track, a second click to previously played track (not necessarily the previous track in the album or playlist); hold down this button and you skip-search back through the currently playing track.
►►I Just like the back skip/rewind button, only forwards.

►II The iPod doesn't have a "stop" button; instead, you simply pause and unpause the music with this button. It also turns the iPod off when held down.

Click wheel tips and tricks

▶ **Scrubbing** This term means speeding through a song visually, rather than aurally. Hit the Select button once to see the current song position. Move forwards or backwards using the scroll wheel and press Select when you are done.

▶ **Now playing** When listening to one track, you can browse through the other tracks and menus as usual. To return to the current playing track choose the option from the Main Menu.

▶ **Rating tracks** Pressing the Select button three times (twice on older models) during playback will allow you to add a star rating to a track (see p.148) using the scroll wheel.

▶ **Making playlists** When browsing through tracks, holding down the Select button for a couple of seconds will allow you to add a highlighted song to the iPod's On-The-Go playlist (see p.144). This can also be done when playing a track by holding down the Select button and choosing the option from the menu that appears.

▶ **About...** To see how much space you have left on the iPod, click About within the Settings menu. This can be unreliable, though, so to be certain, attach your iPod to your computer and take a look at the meter bar, under the Summary tab of the iPod Options panel in iTunes.

▶ **Searching** All current click-wheel iPods allow you to search by song, artist, album, audiobook or podcast. Simply choose Music > Search and use the scroll wheel to enter a search term.

▶ **Genius** On current click-wheel iPods, the Genius feature (see p.134) can be summoned for the currently playing track by either clicking the Select button twice and then using the click wheel to toggle the feature on, or by holding the Select button until the option appears in a new menu. You can also browse for a track to use with the Genius feature and then hold the Select button until the option appears.

Using an iPod touch

Tap the Music icon on the iPod touch home screen and use the buttons at the bottom to browse; by default, these buttons are Songs, Artists, Albums and Playlists. When you have found what you want, tap a name to view the contents or start playing. You can control the volume of the music you are listening to either by using the on-screen slider or, on second-generation touches, the physical buttons on the side of the iPod.

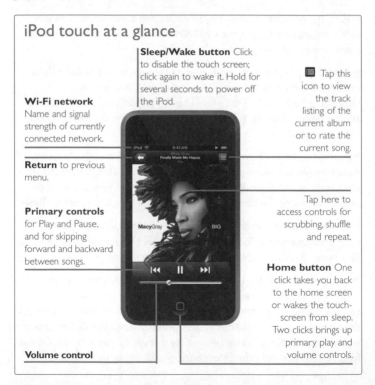

iPod touch at a glance

Sleep/Wake button Click to disable the touch screen; click again to wake it. Hold for several seconds to power off the iPod.

Tap this icon to view the track listing of the current album or to rate the current song.

Wi-Fi network Name and signal strength of currently connected network.

Return to previous menu.

Tap here to access controls for scrubbing, shuffle and repeat.

Primary controls for Play and Pause, and for skipping forward and backward between songs.

Home button One click takes you back to the home screen or wakes the touch-screen from sleep. Two clicks brings up primary play and volume controls.

Volume control

Cover Flow on iPods

Cover Flow allows you to browse your music collection by album artwork. It's long been a feature of iTunes (see p.130) and can now also be found on all new iPod models (except, obviously, the shuffle). On a nano or classic, Cover Flow appears as a menu item within Music, while the nano also displays Cover Flow when rotating through ninety degrees. The iPod touch also shifts into its Cover Flow gear when rotated. The built-in accelerometer of both models recognizes the shift of axis and switches display mode.

To view the track listing of an album in Cover Flow on the touch, either tap its cover or hit ❻, then tap a song in the list to set it playing. On the nano use the scroll wheel and Select button to navigate and make selections.

Touch tips and tricks

▶ **Customize your music browse icons** Click Music > More to reveal further options for browsing your music collection. Depending on your listening habits, you might want to replace the default browse buttons with these. For instance, classical buffs will probably want instant access to Composers, while radio lovers will want to front-load podcasts. To replace an existing browse icon with a different one, tap Edit, and then simply drag the new icon onto the old one. You can also drag the icons at the bottom into any order.

▶ **Scrubbing** To rewind or fast-forward, tap the album artwork of the current track to reveal the "scrubber" bar. Alternatively, press and hold the ◀◀ and ▶▶ controls.

▶ **Sleep** You can have your iPod touch play music, podcasts or videos for a certain amount of time and then switch itself off – like the sleep function of an alarm clock. Tap Clock on the home screen and then Timer, and choose a number of minutes or hours. Then tap When Time Ends, choose Sleep iPod, and hit Start.

▶ **Now playing** Whilst browsing, you can return to the Now Playing screen at any time using the [Now Playing] button.

▶ **Rating tracks** To rate the current track, tap the ▤ icon. Then drag your finger across the five dots near the top of the screen. Your ratings are copied back to iTunes next time you sync, where they can be used in Smart Playlists or to remind you to junk poorly rated tunes.

▶ **Shuffle lists** Whilst browsing your music collection, any list of songs will include a Shuffle option at the top. Click to start a random selection of the current list.

▶ **Genius** To kick start the Genius feature (see p.134) from the Now Playing screen, tap the current selection's cover image and then the ✻ icon that appears below the scrubber bar. The current Genius selections can also be found in the touch's Playlists menu.

More iPod features

You can customize the way an iPod works by tweaking the options in the Settings menus. Following are some of the most useful customizations. Not all of these options apply to all iPods, so explore your model to see what's available:

▶ **Clicks** By default, click-wheel iPods click whenever you touch either the wheel or a button. This will win you no friends when travelling on public transport. To disable the clicks, choose Settings > Clicker.

▶ **Main Menu** Under Settings > Main Menu on a click-wheel iPod, you can choose exactly which browsing categories you want to access from your Pod's top-level menu.

▶ **Screen Lock** Within the Extras menu, Screen Lock lets you set a four-digit code that must be entered every time the iPod wakes from sleep. It's designed to stop people using your iPod without permission, and to keep prying eyes away from private data. If you forget the code, connecting to iTunes will let you unlock, blank and refill the Pod.

▶ **Brightness/Contrast** This can be useful if you're struggling to see the screen. Be warned, though, that a higher brightness or contrast setting will slightly decrease battery life. You can also adjust the brightness on some click-wheel models when watching a movie – click the Select button twice to make the slider appear.

▶**Volume Limiter** If you want to protect your ears or earphones against damage from loud tracks, set a maximum volume level for your iPod. If you're a parent, you may want to set a four-digit combination lock so that your pride and joy can't reset the limit when you're not looking. To enable Volume Limit on an iPod shuffle, connect the Pod to your Mac or PC and look under the Pod's Music tab in iTunes.

▶**Audiobook Speed** Audiobooks recorded in certain file formats can be sped up or slowed down without making the reader sound like a bass-baritone or coloratura soprano.

▶ **Sound Check** This feature enables your iPod to play all tracks at a similar volume level so that none sound either too quiet or too loud. Because these automatic adjustments are pulled across from iTunes, the Sound Check feature also has to be enabled within iTunes. To do this, open Preferences (from the iTunes menu on a Mac and the Edit menu on a PC) then, under the Playback tab tick the Sound Check box.

▶ **EQ** This option lets you assign an equalizer preset to suit your music and earphones. Note that you can also assign EQ settings to individual tracks in iTunes by highlighting them, choosing File > Get Info and then

Crash!

It probably won't be long before your iPod does something strange – such as failing to respond when you press the buttons. In these situations, you'll need to reset your Pod (see p.251) and maybe update your iPod software (see p.251).

looking under the Options tab.

►**Audio Crossfade** This option can be toggled off and on from the Playback menus of current click-wheel iPods.

►**Backlight Timer** This controls how long the screen remains illuminated on a click-wheel iPod after you stop using the controls. Again, a higher setting is more user-friendly but increases battery demands. You can access this setting directly during a photo slideshow (click the Select button once) or during video playback (click the Select button twice).

> **TIP:** Choosing Settings > Reset All Settings will do that and only that – it won't affect any music, video, photos or other data on the Pod.

►**Spoken Menus** Similar to the iPod shuffle's VoiceOver feature (see opposite), the option to have menu items spoken to you can also be enabled from iTunes (but not from the Pod) for current click-wheel iPods. To do this, connect the iPod to your computer and look for the check box under the Pod's Summary tab in iTunes.

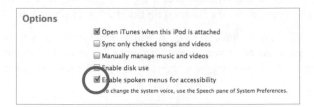

Many of the features listed above can be employed to maximize your iPod's battery life between charges. For more battery tips, see p.254.

Using an iPod shuffle

The third generation iPod shuffle (see p.29) has only one switch on its actual body. This three-way switch controls how the loaded tracks are played back – either shuffled ✖ or played in order ⟳ as they would by default in iTunes. The switch's third position turns the device off.

All other options for controlling the shuffle are managed from a special control unit halfway along the shuffle's earphone cord. As you might expect, the **+** and **−** buttons, found at either end of the control, increase and decrease playback volume respectively. The central recessed "clicker", however, is where you have to master the subtle art of double and triple clicks to get the shuffle to do what you want it to:

▶**Single click** Starts, pauses and resumes playback.

▶**Double click** Takes you to the next track.

▶**Triple click** Takes you to the previous track.

▶**Press and hold** With VoiceOver enabled, this allows you to hear the title and artist of the currently playing track.

▶**Press and hold until the tone, then release** VoiceOver will start to read out the names of all loaded Playlists. When you hear the one you want, click to select.

To make sure that VoiceOver is enabled for your iPod shuffle (see p.47), connect to iTunes, highlight it in the Sources sidebar and then check the box at the bottom of the Summary tab.

> **TIP:** VoiceOver is much more easy to deal with if you keep the labelling of your songs, artists and albums tidy in iTunes. Turn to p.146 to find out how.

Deleting on the go

Many a new iPod user has pulled their hair out trying to delete unwanted music directly from an iPod. The solution is simple: you can't do it on the Pod itself, you have to do it via iTunes. Assuming you have your iPod set to automatically update all songs and playlists, you have a few options:

▶ **Simply delete music from iTunes** (see p.152) and the next time you connect your iPod, the tracks will disappear from there, too.

▶ **Or, if you want the music on iTunes but not on your iPod**, uncheck the little boxes next to the names of the offending tracks, and under the Summary tab of the iPod Options panel tick the "Only update checked songs" box.

▶ **Or, if you don't want to uncheck the songs** (since this will stop them playing in iTunes too), use the manual update option described on p.45 to take more control over exactly what gets transferred to your iPod.

The problem with the above techniques is that you have to remember to delete or uncheck the songs when you get home. If that bothers you, an alternative solution is to instruct iTunes to fill your iPod from a Smart Playlist which includes the criterion "My Rating is not ★".

This way, when you come across a song you want to remove from your iPod, simply rate it with a single star (see p.148). Next time you sync, the ratings will be copied back to iTunes, which will then remove them from your Smart Playlist and Pod.

Importing

04

Importing CDs

Ripping, importing, recording...

Downloading tracks from the Internet is all well and good, but if you already own the CD, there's no point in paying for the same album again. Importing CDs into iTunes is easy, but it's worth reading through this chapter even if you've done it hundreds of times, as various preferences and features are easy to miss. In particular, it's worth considering the various import options, since these determine the sound quality and transferability of the resulting tracks.

> **TIP:** In iTunes Preferences > Importing > On CD Insert you can set iTunes to automatically import and eject each CD that's inserted. This can be very useful if you're ripping a large collection of discs.

To get started, insert any audio CD into your Mac or PC. In most cases, within a few seconds you'll find that the artist, track and album names – and maybe more info besides – automatically appear. This information is not pulled from the CD, which contains nothing but music. Rather, it's downloaded via the Internet from CDDB – a giant CD information database hosted by a company called Gracenote (gracenote.com).

> **TIP:** iTunes can also automatically search for album artwork when you insert a CD. Though you don't pay for the artwork, you will need to have an iTunes Store account (see p.99) set up for this to happen.

If iTunes isn't set to connect to the Net automatically, or your computer is offline, you'll need to tell the program to download the track info from CDDB. Connect to the Internet and then select Get CD Track Names from the Advanced menu in iTunes. If you get no joy from CDDB, the songs will be left with the titles "Track 1", "Track 2" and so on. This happens remarkably infrequently, but it's perfectly likely that the info downloaded will be

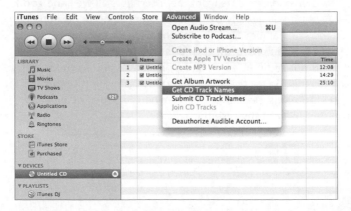

inaccurate or won't tally with your own ideas of music categoriza-
tion – one person's hip-hop is another's R&B, after all. In either
case, you'll need to edit the information manually, either before or
after you import them. See p.146 to find out how.

TIP: If you rip a few CDs to a laptop when you're out
and about and can't get online, you can always
access the CDDB database later. Simply select the track or tracks
in question (searching for "track" should find them quickly) and
click Get CD Track Names from the Advanced menu.

Joining tracks

Before importing the tracks from a CD it's
possible to "join" some of them together.
Then, when they're played back on your
computer or your iPod, they'll always stay
together as one unit, and iTunes won't
insert a gap between the tracks. This is
useful if you have an album in which two
or more tracks are segued together (the
end of one song merging into the begin-

▲	Song Name
1	☑ ┌ Mara
2	│ Timo M
3	│ Phaser
4	│ Danny
5	│ Sandra
6	└ Stef

ning of the next) or if you just think certain tracks should always
be heard together (if you joined the three movements of a symphony, for example, the whole work will appear together when
you're playing in Shuffle mode).

Simply select the tracks you want to join and then click Join
CD Tracks from the Advanced menu. In the short term you can

TIP: iTunes only allows you to join tracks before
you import. Mac users who want to join
them after importing should seek out Track Splicer from
Doug's AppleScripts (dougscripts.com/itunes).

change your mind by clicking Unjoin CD Tracks, but once you've pressed the Import CD button, the songs will be imported as a single audio file that cannot be separated without the use of audio-editing software (see p.73).

Importing…

OK, now you've sorted out the track details and file format, it's time to import your CD's songs into the iTunes Library. To the left of each song title in the Song List you'll see a checked tick-box; if you don't wish to import a particular track from a CD, uncheck its box. Now hit the Import CD button in the lower-right corner of the iTunes window and watch as each of your selections is copied to your iTunes Library.

Choosing the right settings

Before importing all your music, have a look through the various Importing options, which you'll find behind the Import Settings button on the General pane of iTunes Preferences. These are worth considering early on, as they relate to sound quality and compatibility: you don't want to have to re-rip all your CDs a few months down the line if you decide that you're not happy with the sound, or you want to use the tracks with an MP3 player that doesn't support Apple's default AAC format.

MP3, AAC and other import options

MP3 [Moving Pictures Experts Group-1/2 Audio Layer 3]
MP3 is the most common format for storing music on computer and digital
music players – by quite a long way. That gives it one great advantage: if you
import your music as MP3s, you can be safe in the knowledge that it will be
transferable to any other player or software you might use in the future, or which
friends and family may already own. However, it no longer provides the best
sound-quality/disk-space balance.
File name ends: .mp3
Use it for: importing music you want to be able to share with non-iPod people
and players, and for burning CDs to play on special MP3 CD players.

AAC [Advanced Audio Coding]
This is the encoding format that is being pushed by Apple for two reasons. First,
according to the general consensus, AAC sounds noticeably better than MP3
when recorded at the same bitrate. Second, AAC is the file format used for all
audio files downloaded from the iTunes Store. In fact, the two import settings for
AAC files offered by default in iTunes are also the two encoding settings available
in the iTunes Store: 128kbps and 256kbps (aka iTunes Plus).
File name ends: .m4a (standard), **.m4p** (when DRM is included)
Use it for: importing music you don't expect to share with non-iPod people
and players.

Apple Lossless Encoder
A recent Apple innovation, this format offers full CD quality, but only consumes
around half the disk space – expect to fit between three and five albums per
gigabyte. Currently the format only works on iTunes and iPods.
File name ends: .ale
Use it for: importing music at the highest quality for computer or iPod use.
Note, though, that it won't work with an iPod shuffle.

AIFF [Advanced Interchange File Format], **WAV** [Wave]
These uncompressed formats offer the same quality as the newer Apple Lossless
Encoder but they take up twice as much disk space (and won't play back on an
iPod shuffle). In their favour, they can be played on nearly any computer software
and also imported into audio-editing programs. Also, you might find that CDs
import slightly more quickly than with Apple Lossless.
File name ends: .aiff, .wav
Use it for: importing music for burning onto CD and then deleting, or for editing with audio software, but not for general iTunes or Pod playback.

Which format?

iTunes currently offers five file-format import options: AAC, MP3, AIFF, Apple Lossless and WAV. The box on the previous page explains the pros, cons and uses of each format. But, in brief, AAC is best for day-to-day iPod and computer use; MP3 is slightly worse at the same bitrate, but can be played on any digital music player or computer (and burned onto MP3 CDs); Apple Lossless is for fidelity fanatics; and AIFF and WAV are only really for importing tracks with the aim of burning CDs.

Note that all file formats can be burned to audio CDs and played back in normal hi-fis – it's only when sharing actual music files with non-iTunes or non-iPod equipment that compatibility becomes an issue.

LAME MP3 encoding

Just as there's more than one way to skin a cat, there's also more than one way to encode an MP3 file. The encoder built into iTunes does a decent-enough job, but there are alternatives out there that arguably do it better. Indeed, there's a near-consensus among people who are interested in such things that the best MP3 encoder for files with a bitrate of 128kbps or higher is an open-source (non-copyrighted) one known as LAME. (Its somewhat self-deprecating name stands, bizarrely enough, for "LAME Ain't an MP3 Encoder".)

Mac users who fancy getting the audiophile benefits of LAME can grab the easy-to-use "iTunes-LAME" script (*blacktree.com/apps/iTunes-LAME*), which adds LAME encoding to iTunes via the Scripts menu. Once installed, you can use LAME when importing tracks from a CD, and also when converting songs into MP3 from other formats. If you have a PC, you'll find various free programs featuring LAME encoding at *lame.sourceforge.net/links.html*, though at the time of writing none of them integrate quite so neatly with iTunes.

Which bitrate?

As already explained (see p.23), the bitrate is the amount of data that each second of sound is reduced to. The higher the bitrate, the higher the sound quality, but also the more disk space the track takes up. The relationship between file size and bitrate is basically proportional, but the same isn't true of sound quality, so a 128kbps track takes half as much space as the same track recorded at 256kbps, but the sound will be only very marginally different. Still, marginal differences are what being a hi-fi obsessive is all about.

Running a soundcheck

The only reliable way to determine the right sound quality for your own ear, headphones and hi-fi is to do a comparative experiment. Launch iTunes and insert a CD you consider to be as detailed and clear in its recording quality as anything in your collection. Pick one track that sounds particularly hi-fi and uncheck the rest of the tracks. Name it "Soundcheck ALE" in the Song List, since you will be importing this at CD quality using Apple Lossless format. Open iTunes Preferences and select the Apple Lossless option within Advanced/Importing. Import the track.

Next, return to the CD in the Sources sidebar, rename the track "Soundcheck 128 AAC", select the AAC 128kbps option from Preferences, and import the track again. Do this again at various other AAC and/or MP3 bitrates – say 160, 224 and 320kbps – each time renaming the track so it's easy to locate.

Song Name ▲	Bit Rate	Artist	Time	Album
☑ Mozart Sound Check – 128 ACC	128 kbps	Hagen Quartet	5:47	Mozart Selected Quartets
☑ Mozart Sound Check – 160 ACC	160 kbps	Hagen Quartet	5:47	Mozart Selected Quartets
☑ Mozart Sound Check – 192 ACC	192 kbps	Hagen Quartet	5:47	Mozart Selected Quartets
☑ Mozart Sound Check – 224 ACC	224 kbps	Hagen Quartet	5:47	Mozart Selected Quartets
☑ Mozart Sound Check – AIFF	1411 kbps	Hagen Quartet	5:47	Mozart Selected Quartets

Once you're done, plug in your iPod, transfer the tracks across, and then do some comparative listening either on headphones or, ideally, connected through a decent home stereo and speaker system (see p.176). Then you can make an informed decision about which format is right for you.

The default import setting in recent versions of iTunes, listed as "high quality", is AAC at 128kbps. Most people will be perfectly satisfied with this combination (which is usually said to be roughly equivalent to MP3 at 160kbps), but if you're into your sound in a serious way it may not be quite good enough. Particularly if you listen to high-fidelity recordings of acoustic instruments, such as well-recorded classical music, and if you connect your iPod or computer to a decent home stereo (see p.176) you may find AAC 128kbps leads to a distinct lack of presence and brightness in your favourite recordings. If so, either opt for the Apple Lossless Encoder (see p.65) or stick with AAC and up the bitrate. The best thing to do is to run a comparative experiment with a suitably well-recorded track (see box on previous page).

TIP: One problem with bigger, higher-quality music files is that, when played on an iPod, they use slightly more battery power each second when played.

Tweaking the settings

When setting the bitrate, the Custom option reveals a panel full of techie settings relating to frequencies and the like. You can safely ignore most of these, though it's worth knowing about one or two, as they may help you to strike a better balance between file size and sound quality.

Channels

With mono encoding there is only one "channel" of music within the file, which, when played, is duplicated to both your left and right earphones or speakers. Stereo encoding produces a two-channel file, which gives you a distinct sound in both left and right speakers and creates file sizes double those of mono. The

Joint Stereo option reduces the file size of normal stereo slightly by combining parts of the two channels where possible. Podcasts (see p.118) are often encoded in either mono or joint stereo to keep their file size down.

Variable Bit Rate Encoding

When switched on, VBR varies the bitrate in real time, according to the complexity of the sound. With some music, this can save quite a lot of disk space.

Smart Encoding Adjustments

If you select Smart Encoding Adjustments, then iTunes will automatically select what it thinks are the most appropriate settings for any options you've left set to Auto.

Filter Frequencies Below 10Hz

Frequencies below 10Hz are inaudible to humans, so removing them should reduce the size of your files without affecting the sound. But try a test file before making this your default setting, as some audiophiles have commented that removing these frequencies can result in an unbalanced sound and even the appearance of a tinnitus-like ringing in the recording.

Combining different formats

It's fine to mix different file formats and bitrates in your Library. Indeed, this is a sensible plan as some kinds of music will receive little benefit from high-bitrate encoding. Very sludgy, stoner-type rock, for example, may not require the same fidelity as a carefully regulated Fazioli grand piano.

If you're a hi-fi buff with plenty of computer disk space, consider importing your CDs using Apple Lossless for use through your stereo (see p.67) but creating an AAC copy of each for use on your iPod, where disk space is more limited. After you've created the copies, simply create a Smart Playlist (see p.141) that finds all MP3 and AAC files, and set your Pod to automatically update that playlist only (see p.45).

05

Importing vinyl & cassettes

... and other analogue sound sources

If you have the time and inclination, it's perfectly possible to connect to your hi-fi with the goal of importing music from an analogue sound source such as vinyl, cassette or radio, and then import the music into iTunes and onto your iPod. For vinyl, the easiest option is to buy a USB turntable, such as those from Ion or Kam (pictured overleaf), but this isn't strictly necessary. With the right cables, you can connect your hi-fi, Walkman, MiniDisc-player or any other source to your computer and do it manually.

Stage 1: Hooking up

First of all, you'll need to
make the right connec-
tion. With any luck,
your computer will
have a line-in or
mic port, probably
in the form of a
minijack socket (if
it doesn't you can
add one with the
right audio interface;
see box opposite). On
the hi-fi, a headphone
socket will suffice, but
you'll get a
better "level" from a
dedicated line-out –
check on the back of
the system for a pair

A USB
turntable, such as
this one from KAM, allows
you to record vinyl onto your
computer without worrying about audio
interfaces and editing software. If you've got a huge
archive of vinyl to rip, they can be a lifesaver, but for a
few records they aren't worth the investment. It might
be cheaper to buy the albums again from iTunes.

of RCA sockets labelled "Line Out", "Tape Out" or something similar. Depending on whether you're connecting to a headphone jack
or a pair of RCA sockets, you'll either need minijack-to-minijack
cable or an RCA-to-minijack cable (see p.177).

> **TIP:** If you're setting up a turntable especially to
> record into iTunes, make sure you connect it to a
> stereo amplifier through a dedicated "phono" port. Otherwise,
> you'll need a separate preamplifier, since vinyl is often cut with
> bass and treble frequencies reversed to decrease the need for
> an overly wide and deep groove. Preamplifiers and phono ports
> correct this inverted equalization, boost the levels, and generally
> stop the signal sounding tinny.

Audio interfaces

Though most computers do feature line-in sockets, some – such as Apple's iBook – don't. But there are loads of pieces of USB hardware on the market that will provide you with a basic line-in and mic-in socket (such as Griffin's iMic, pictured) or, if your budget allows, a more professional selection of studio-quality ports and sockets, such as those made by M-Audio.

iMic griffintechnology.com/products/imic
M-Audio m-audio.com

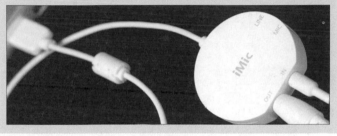

Stage 2: Check you have enough disk space

During the actual recording process, you'll need plenty of hard-drive space: as much as a gigabyte for an album, or 15MB per minute. Once you've finished recording, you can convert the music you've imported into a space-efficient format such as MP3 or AAC (see p.65), and delete the giant originals.

Stage 3: Choose some software

Recording from an analogue source requires an audio-editing application. You may already have something suitable on your computer, but there are also scores of excellent programs available to download off the Internet.

Our recommendations would be GarageBand for Mac users, which anyone with an Apple machine purchased in the last few

years will already have, and Audacity, which is available for both
PC and Mac, is easy to use and totally free:

Audacity audacity.sourceforge.net
GarageBand apple.com/garageband

For many more audio software options, including freebies, point
your Web browser at:

AudioMelody audiomelody.com
Shareware Music Machine hitsquad.com/smm
Tucows tucows.com

> **TIP:** Audio-editing software isn't just for recording. It
> can also come in useful for trimming, cutting up,
> editing or combining tracks from your iTunes Library.

Stage 4: Recording…

Connect your computer and hi-fi as described above, and switch your hi-fi's amplifier to "Phono", "Tape" or whichever channel you're recording from. Launch your audio recorder and open a new file. The details from here on vary according to which program you're running and the analogue source you are recording from, but roughly speaking the procedure is the same.

You'll be asked to specify a few parameters for the new recording. The defaults (usually 44.1kHz, 16-bit stereo) should be fine. Play the loudest section of the record to get an idea of the maximum level. A visual meter should display the sound coming in – you want as much level as possible *without* hitting the red.

If you seem to be getting little or no level, make sure your line-in is specified as your recording channel and the input volume is up: on a Mac, look under Sound in System Preferences; on a PC, look in Control Panel.

When you're ready, press "Record" and start your vinyl, cassette or other source playing. When the song or album is finished, press "Stop". A graphic wave form will appear on the screen. Use the "cut" tool to tidy up any extraneous noise or blank space from the beginning and end of the file; fade in and out to hide the "cuts", and, if you like, experiment with any hiss, pop and crackle filters on offer.

Stage 5: Tidying up the sound

It won't always be necessary, but it's often a good idea – especially if you're recording from vinyl – to try to clean up the sound a bit. Your audio editor may offer hiss, pop and crackle filters, or for serious projects you could try a dedicated noise-reduction program, such as SoundSoap (bias-inc.com). However, don't go clean-up mad and don't overwrite your original file until you get just the right sound: removing hiss and crackle is good, but if you end up with a recording that lacks the warmth or presence of the shellac version, you'll be disappointed.

If there's a "normalize" function you could also use this to maximize the level without distorting it. This will ensure that, if you rip a number of tracks, they will all end up at the same volume level.

Stage 6: Drop it into iTunes

When you are happy with what you've got, save the file in WAV or AIFF format, drag it into iTunes and convert it to AAC or MP3 by choosing the Import settings under the Advanced tab of iTunes

TIP: If you use GarageBand, you can export directly to iTunes from the Share menu. You can then either send the track at maximum quality (which will generate a very large file size) or check the Compress box to tinker with the various compression and format options.

Preferences and then choosing the Convert… command from the iTunes Advanced menu. Finally, delete the bulky original of the track from both your iTunes folder and its original location.

Read on

The finer details of recording and editing audio can take a lifetime to master. If you want good results, or you get stuck, do some reading online, starting with:

OSXAudio osxaudio.com
PC Music Guru pc-music.com

06

Importing photos

Pictures in your pocket

he iPod isn't going to revolutionize photography in the same way it and other MP3 players have revolutionized listening to music. That said, iPod screens are vividly luscious, and getting digital images from your computer into your pocket has never been easier. And if you have an iPod touch, you have the added joy of grabbing images off  the Web; and let's not forget the stack of extra apps available for playing with the images you have stored in your touch's belly.

Syncing pictures through iTunes

Whether you use a Mac or PC, it's iTunes that handles the task of moving pictures from your computer to your iPod. It can move images over from any standard folders – such as the My Pictures folder in Windows, or the Pictures folder in OS X – but you might prefer to use iTunes in conjunction with a program that lets you arrange your photos into albums. At the time of writing, only a handful of programs are supported:

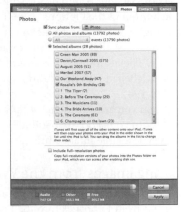

iPhoto (Mac) apple.com/iphoto (bundled with all new Macs)
Aperture (Mac) apple.com/aperture ($199/£126)
Photoshop Elements (PC) adobe.com/photoshopelements ($90/£60)
Photoshop Album (PC) adobe.com (supported, but discontinued)

To get things started, connect your iPod to your computer and select its icon. In the Options area, click the Photos tab and choose the source of your photos from the dropdown menu. The My Pictures and Pictures folders will appear in this list by default on PC and Mac respectively, as will any compatible photo-management programs installed on your system (if your images are elsewhere use the Choose Folder option to browse for them). At the bottom of the window you will see a running total of how many pics you have selected to sync.

> **TIP:** iPods support JPEGs, BMPs, GIFs, TIFFs and PNGs. If a photo doesn't display, make sure it's in one of these formats. If not, re-save it.

During the sync process iTunes creates re-sized, space-efficient versions of your originals for your iPod to use. Check the box at the bottom of the Options pane if you additionally want to copy the higher-quality originals to your iPod, so that you can print them or pass them on to friends and family when away from home. They can then be accessed from the Photos folder in a sub-folder labelled Full Resolution when your iPod is Disk use enabled (see p.190).

When you are done, click Apply and the photos will wing their way onto your Pod. Be patient, this can take a while the first time you sync a large image library.

Saving images from the Web

iPod touch users have the additional option of saving photos and images from webpages into the Pod's photo folders whilst surfing via Wi-Fi. When you find an image that you want to keep, simply press and hold it on the screen until the Save Image option appears. It is exactly the same process for saving images that have been emailed to you (see p.198). Next time your iPod is synced, you are prompted to move images harvested in this way to your computer.

Connecting to a TV

All colour-screen iPods that can play video files on their screens can be connected to TVs via an AV cable (available separately). A minijack plug connects directly to the Pod, and three colour-coded plugs (red and white for sound, yellow for pictures) connect to the TV. Next, turn to your iPod and check that the TV-out signal is enabled and specify whether your TV requires NTSC (US) or PAL (Europe) signals. You'll find these options under Photos > Settings on a click-wheel iPod and within Settings > Video on an iPod touch.

Note that iPods struggle to display very large slideshows via a TV, so try to avoid albums that contain more than around two hundred images.

View images on your Pod

Once your images are synced across, photo navigation is intuitive and requires little elaboration. Here's the very least you need to know:

▶**On a click-wheel iPod** Choose Photo from the top-level menu, then browse and make selections just as you would songs. To kick-start a slideshow, use the ▶II button (if you have an album selected) or the Select button (if you're already viewing a single image). For playback options, explore the Photos > Settings menu.

▶**On an iPod touch** Tap the sunflower icon on the Home screen and you're away. Tapping the image you are currently viewing toggles the control strips on and off and you simply swipe to move between shots. To start a slideshow, tap the ▶ icon on the lower control strip; slideshow preferences can be found within Settings > Photos. Also, take a moment to tap the 🖻 icon. This lets you do things such as set an image as your iPod's wallpaper or email a photo to a friend.

Photo apps

The App Store (see p.119) features loads of great third-party apps to add image manipulation features to the iPod touch. Be careful though, as many such apps are often aimed at iPhones (which have built-in cameras); always check both hardware and firmware compatibility before you download. To get started, click the Store's Photography category, or search for one of these:

▶**Panoramas** A great app for stitching together multiple images from a photo library to create a seamless panorama. ($1.99/£1.19)

▶**My New Smile** Rather than paying an arm and a leg to go to the dentist, use this app to replace your teeth in photos with a lovely new set. (free)

▶**Flickit** The best of many apps in the Store for posting images to Flickr.com. You need to be in range of a Wi-Fi network to get this to work. (free)

▶**Scribble Lite** This is a lovely little app for sketching little pics using the iPod touch. Lots of fun and great for kids. (free)

07

Importing DVDs & video files

How to download or roll your own

All current iPods with screens are video-capable. While such small screens pose no great threat to televisions, being able to play music videos, TV shows, home movies and even DVDs on your Pod is occasionally useful – and often fun.

Just as with music, before you can transfer video to your iPod, you first have to get them into iTunes. This might mean importing existing video files, ripping DVDs or recording from TV. Let's look at each of these options in turn…

Importing existing files

If you have some video files on your computer and you want to get them onto your Pod, you first need to convert them to an iPod-compatible format. In most cases (with MOV, MPEG and MP4 files) this is as simple as dragging the file into your iTunes library, highlighting them and then selecting Convert iPod or iPhone Version from the iTunes Advanced menu. Once that's done, you can delete the older file from iTunes (check the Date Added column in the Song List to be sure which is which).

With certain video files, you may find that they will either not convert in iTunes, or not even import into iTunes in the first place. In these cases, you need to grab some extra software to help you convert the files to the necessary format:

QuickTime Pro apple.com/quicktime/pro (PC and Mac)
This Pro version, which costs $30/£20, is the advanced version of Apple's free media player and can handle most video file types (though not Windows Media files). Once you have your video file open in

QuickTime, simply press Export in the File menu
and choose the "Movie to iPod" option. Take
the resulting file and drag it onto the Library
icon in iTunes.

Video2Go onlymac.de/indexe.html (Mac only)
This $10 application is even simpler than
QuickTime Pro. It lets you browse for video
files already on your Mac, then handles the con-
version and drops the converted files straight into your iTunes Library.

ffmpegX homepage.mac.com/major4 (Mac only)
This intimidatingly named tool (which is free to download and use
but requests a $15 fee from those who like and use it) gives complete
control over various file format settings. However, to get it working
you'll need to install a couple of other free files and mess about a bit
with a few settings. For a clear tutorial, see:
arstechnica.com/guides/tweaks/ipod-video.ars/3

Video formats

Video files are more confusing than most, as you have to worry not only about
the file format (which you can usually tell by the file extension: eg .mov and .avi)
but also the "codec" (compression technique) used to create the file. To make
things even more complex, various other factors – such as frames per second
and audio formats – may also affect whether a particular file can play back on a
particular piece of hardware or software.

In short, the video-capable iPods available at the time of writing support files in
the .m4v, .mp4 and .mov formats created using H.264 and MPEG-4 codecs. In full,
the supported video specifications are as follows:

▶ **H.264 video** up to 2.5Mbps, 640 × 480, 30 frames per second, Baseline Profile
up to Level 3.0 with AAC-LC audio up to 160kbps, 48 kHz, stereo audio .m4v,
.mp4, and .mov file formats.

▶ **MPEG-4 video** up to 2.5 Mbps, 640 × 480, 30 frames per second, Simple
Profile with AAC-LC audio up to 160kbps, 48kHz, stereo audio in .m4v, .mp4, and
.mov file formats.

Importing DVDs

In most cases, it's perfectly possible to get DVDs onto your iPod. In some countries this may not be strictly legal when it comes to copyrighted movies, but as long as you're only importing your own DVDs for your own use, no one is likely to mind. The main problem is that it's a bit of a hassle. A DVD contains so much data that it can take more than an hour to "rip" each movie to your computer in a format that'll work with iTunes and an iPod. And if the disc contains copy protection (see below), then it's even more of a headache.

DVD copy protection

DVDs are often encrypted, or copy protected, to stop people making copies or ripping the discs to their computers. PC owners can use a program such as AnyDVD (*slysoft.com*) to get around the protection, while Mac owners trying to get encrypted DVDs onto their iPods will need to grab a program such as Fast DVD Copy (*fastdvdcopy.com*). This allows you to make a non-protected copy of the movie, which you can then get onto your iPod in the standard way. For more on this process, and other applications that do the job, see *The Rough Guide to Macs & OS X*. Note that, in some countries, it may not be legal to copy an encrypted DVD.

Using HandBrake

Of the various free tools available for getting DVDs into iTunes, ready for transfer to an iPod, probably the best is HandBrake, which is available for both Mac and PC. Here's how the process works:

▶ **Download and install HandBrake** from handbrake.com.

▶ **Insert the DVD** and, if it starts to play automatically, quit your DVD player program.

►**Launch HandBrake** and it should detect the DVD (it may call it something unfriendly like "/dev/rdisk1"). Press Open, and wait until the application has scanned the DVD.

►**Choose iPod-friendly settings**
Choose one of the two iPod options from the Presets menu.

►**Check the source**
It's also worth taking a quick look at the "Title" dropdown menu within the Source section of HandBrake. If the list offers several options, choose the one that represents the largest amount of time (for example 01h22m46s) as this should be the main feature. If nothing of an appropriate length appears, then your DVD is copy protected (see p.85).

> **TIP:** If you check the "2-pass encoding" box, this will double the process time, but the quality will be better, and with no increase in the size of the final file.

►**Subtitles** If it's a foreign-language film, set Dialogue and Subtitles options from the dropdown menus behind the Audio & Subtitles tab.

►**Rip** Hit the Start button at the bottom of the window and the encoding will begin. Don't hold your breath.

►**Drop the file into iTunes** Unless you choose to save it somewhere else, the file will eventually appear on the Desktop. It will probably be in the region of a few hundred megabytes, depending on

Recording from TV

If you want to be able to record from TV to iPod, you'll need a TV receiver for your computer. Some posh PCs have these built in, but if yours doesn't you should be able to pick one up relatively inexpensively, and attach it to your PC or Mac via USB or FireWire.

As usual, things are easiest for Mac users, thanks to Elgato's superb EyeTV range of portable TV receivers, some of which are as small as an iPod. With an EyeTV, it's easy to record TV shows and then export them directly into an iPod-friendly format. For more info, see:

Elgato *elgato.com*

PC users have many brands of TV receiver/recorders available, though at the time of writing none allows you to export directly in an iPod-friendly format. Instead, record the shows in any format of your choice and use QuickTime Pro to re-save them for the iPod.

> **TIP:** If your home-recorded iPod videos display horizontal lines during playback, try locating and enabling a "deinterlace" option in whichever program you're using to save them into an iPod-friendly format.

the length of the DVD. Drag the file into the main iTunes window. This should create a copy of the new file in your iTunes library (see p.153 to make sure you have iTunes set to do this) allowing you to then delete the original file from your Desktop.

Other tools

There are various other DVD-ripping programmes out there. One good choice for PCs is ImTOO DVD-to-iPod Converter.

ImTOO imtoo.com/dvd-to-ipod-converter.html ($29)

For a few dollars more you could try out Xilisoft's DVD-to-iPod Suite, which guides you through the process in simple step-by-step style.

Xilisoft DVD to iPod Suite xilisoft.com

... and onto the iPod

Once you've assembled some iPod-friendly videos, connect your iPod and highlight it in the Sources sidebar. Then, check the files are selected under either the Movies or TV Shows tab of your iPod's Options panel and hit Apply to move the files onto your iPod.

Once on the iPod, all movies and TV shows appear under "Videos". Unwatched shows and video podcasts appear with a blue dot next to them in the list. From here they can be controlled just like songs, while the iPod touch screen offers the following additional controls:

▶ **Double-tap** the screen to toggle full-screen and theatrical widescreen modes.

▶ **Single-tap** the screen to reveal play, pause, volume and scrubbing controls.

For advice on playing videos from your iPod through a television, turn to p.181.

TIP: Don't forget that the iPod touch comes with a built-in YouTube player to access online video clips over Wi-Fi. Tap the YouTube icon on the Home screen to explore.

08

Importing from other computers

… via iPod, CD or network

I t's often useful to copy audio and video files from one computer to another, and from there onto your iPod. Perhaps you have music spread across more than one Mac or PC, and you want to create a single complete collection. Or perhaps you want to grab files from a friend. Of course, importing a huge archive of copyrighted music from a friend's Mac or PC would be legally dodgy, but you might want to copy tracks they've recorded themselves, for example. Here's how.

Copying the files

One way to import music from other computers is to set your
iPod to manual mode, as described on p.45. However, it's far preferable to actually copy the relevant music files from one computer
to the other. This way they'll be safely backed up on PC or Mac
and you won't lose them if you turn off manual mode or find
yourself with a lost or damaged iPod.

There are three main ways to copy the tracks across:

▶ **On a hard drive or iPod** If you have an external hard drive or
key drive, connect it and drag the tracks from iTunes onto its icon.
Alternatively, locate the files in Finder or Windows and drag them
from there. If you don't have an external drive but you do have an
iPod, you could enable Disk use on the iPod (see p.190) and use it to
copy across the files in just the same way.

Note that, if copying between a Mac and PC, you'll need to use a
hard drive or iPod formatted by a PC (not by a Mac).

If you're having
any trouble
dragging tracks
straight out
of iTunes, try
locating the
files in Finder
or Windows
and copy them
from there.

▶ **On CD or DVD** If you're copying from a computer with iTunes,
follow the instructions in Chapter 17 to create a data CD (up to ten
hours of music files) or data DVD (more like sixty hours).

▶ **Over a network** If the computers in question are already on the same network, you can enable file sharing and simply copy the artist folders you want directly from one machine to another. File sharing may already be on: if not, on a Mac, open System Preferences and look under Sharing; on a PC, right-click the iTunes folder and select Sharing and Security. For more details, search Windows or Mac OS X Help.

Importing the files

Before importing the files into iTunes on the second computer, first make sure the program is set to copy the files into the correct place, rather than leaving them where they currently are (ie on a hard disk, DVD or your desktop). To do this, open Preferences from the iTunes or Edit menu and click the Advanced button.

Under the General tab make sure that the "Copy files to iTunes Music folder when adding to library" box is checked.

Once that's done, simply copy the files or folders straight into the main iTunes window – or onto a specific playlist icon if you like. The same thing can be achieved by choosing the Add to Library command from the File menu.

File format issues

Of course, you can only import files in formats that iTunes can recognize. At present, that includes the ones mentioned in the previous chapter – AAC, MPS, Apple Loseless, AIFF and WAV – in addition to non-protected Windows Media files (.wma) and Audible (.aa), a special format designed for spoken-word recordings and eBooks.

If you stumble upon files that iTunes can't import you may find that you can easily convert them into an iTunes-friendly format with the help of a downloadable tool such as:

dBpoweramp Music Converter
dbpoweramp.com (PC; $28)
Dubbed by its makers as the "Swiss army knife of Audio", dMC is easy to use and can convert pretty much any file format you might come across.

Fluke
code.google.com/p/flukeformac (Mac; Free)
Handy little script for importing otherwise-unplayable FLAC files into iTunes.

SoundConverter dekorte.com/projects/shareware/SoundConverter (Mac; $10)
A good choice for Mac users. Simply choose your output option from the dropdown menus and then drag-and-drop the files you want to convert.

Xiph QuickTime Component
xiph.org/quicktimeformat
Allows you to play Ogg Vorbis files (see box below) within iTunes.

Ogg Vorbis and open-source formats

Terms like MP3 are so ubiquitous that it's easy to assume that they're common property, but in fact nearly all such technologies are the intellectual assets of companies, which charge other companies (such as software manufacturers) to use them. Somewhere along the line, consumers foot the bill and profits may come before other considerations.

Increasingly, however, where there's a commercial piece of software there's also a free alternative produced by the open-source programming community (best known for the Linux operating system). And, true to form, the open-source crew have developed their own "patent-and-royalty-free" music file format: Ogg Vorbis (.ogg). This format is often claimed to sound better than any other format (visit *vorbis.com* if you "dare to compare").

At the time of writing, Apple hasn't included Ogg Vorbis support on the iPod. If you'd like to see them do so, drop Apple a line and let them know. In the meantime, it is possible to get Ogg Vorbis files to work within iTunes using the QuickTime Component mentioned on the previous page, or by converting them to another format.

Downloads

09

The iTunes Store

The Apple option

As the following chapters show, the iTunes Store isn't the only option for downloading music and video from the Internet. But if you use iTunes and an iPod, it's unquestionably the most convenient, offering instant, legal access to millions of tracks, plus a growing selection of TV shows and movies, to either buy or rent. You can even find some movies on offer in HD. Unlike some of its competitors, the iTunes Store is not a website, so don't expect to reach it with Internet Explorer or Safari. The only ways in are through iTunes – click the Store icon in the Sources sidebar – or via the iTunes icon on an iPod touch or iPhone.

What have they got?

At the time of writing, the iTunes Store boasts more than ten million tracks worldwide, plus twenty thousand audiobooks and a large and growing selection of videos, movies and TV shows. It claims to have the largest legal download catalogue in the world.

However, there are some glaring omissions, and it isn't like a regular shop where anything can be ordered if you're prepared to wait a while. As with any download site, everything that's up there is the result of a deal struck with the record label in question, and several independent record distributors have refused to sign up. So don't expect to find everything you want.

That said, thousands of new tracks appear week after week, so the situation can only get better. And there are plenty of other places to look if you can't find what you want – see p.105.

DRM, sound quality & iTunes Plus

All tracks in the iTunes Store are available in the so-called iTunes Plus format (AAC at 256kbps). This format comes with no built-in DRM of the kind that used to be found in the lower quality (AAC at 128kbps) iTunes-purchased files (see p.18) that the Store stopped selling in spring 2009.

Without the built-in DRM there are no technological barriers to someone distributing the files they have purchased. However, files downloaded from the iTunes Store do contain the purchaser's name and email details embedded as "metadata" within the file. The upshot of this is that files purchased from iTunes and then illegally distributed over the Internet are traceable back to the person who originally shelled out for them. The other thing worth noting about iTunes-purchased files is that they're still in the AAC format (see p.65), so they'll only play in iTunes, on iPods, iPhones and any non-Apple software and hardware which supports this type of file; unless, of course, you convert them to MP3 first (see p.65).

If your library contains any iTunes-purchases in the older, lower-bitrate format, you can pay a small charge to repurchase the tracks in the newer iTunes Plus format – ie, better sound quality and no DRM. On the Store's homepage look for the "Upgrade to iTunes Plus" link in the right-hand panel to find out more.

Logging in for the first time

Though any iTunes user can browse the iTunes Store, listen to samples and look at artwork, if you actually want to buy anything you need to set up an account. This is easily done: hit the Sign In button; press Create New Account (or choose, if you prefer, to use your existing MobileMe or AOL account details); and follow the prompts to enter your payment and contact details. If someone else is already signed in to the Store on the same computer, they'll need to sign out first.

Though iTunes can be set to remember your password for purchases, this could be asking for trouble (especially if you have kids who use iTunes on your machine, see p.102). It is far safer to keep your password private and enter it each time you want to buy something.

Navigating

You shouldn't struggle to find your way around the iTunes Store.
Like online CD stores such as Amazon, it lets you peruse by genre,
look at staff favourites, featured artists, exclusives and so on. But
it also lets you use the various tools familiar from browsing your
own iTunes collection. For example:

Searching

Once you are in the store, the iTunes Search field can be used to
search the Store's catalogue. The homepage also features a link to
"Power Search" where you can narrow your search criteria.

> **TIP:** Use the ⌘ key (Mac) or Ctrl key (Windows) in
> conjunction with the square-bracket keys to go
> back and forth between iTunes Store windows.

Browsing

The browse function works in exactly the same way as it does for
your own library: hit the Browse link in the top-right panel to display genre, artist and album columns.

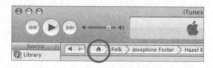

You can go "up a level", or
right back to the Store's
homepage, by clicking the
arrowed tabs at the top.

Quicklinks

You can use the little grey Quicklink buttons next to
track details to view all the Store's selections for the artist
in question. Quicklinks can be turned off for songs you
already own in iTunes Preferences > General.

Previewing

You can preview thirty seconds' worth of any track or video within the iTunes Store catalogue by double-clicking it or selecting it and pressing the play button.

You can also drag any previews into playlists to listen to later (pictured).

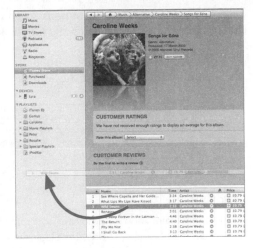

TIP: Just like any other item in the Sources sidebar, double-clicking the iTunes Store's icon opens it in a separate window.

Buying

Once you're ready to buy a song, movie or TV show, there are two ways to go about it. You could use the "1-Click" method, whereby a single click of a Buy Song button in the Song List will debit the payment from your card and start the track downloading.

Alternatively you can shop using the Shopping Cart, which appears in the Sources sidebar. This way, you browse the store and add tracks to

your cart, using the Add Song buttons; when you are done, click the cart's icon, check its contents and hit the Buy Now button to pay and download.

You can set which method you wish to use in the iTunes Preferences panel – look under the Store tab.

> **TIP:** If you want to stop your kids either accessing the iTunes Store entirely or having their tender ears exposed to explicit material, look for the options under the Parental tab of iTunes Preferences.

Renting

Many of the major movie studios are now making their films (both new releases and catalogue titles) available for rental via the iTunes Store. Some titles are additionally made available in HD with a slightly higher rental cost. Once a rented movie file has been down-loaded to your iTunes library you have thirty days to start watching it, and once you have played even just a few seconds of the file, you have twenty-four hours to finish it. When your time runs out the file miraculously disappears from your system. At the time of writing, the iTunes Store rental selection is pretty thin on the ground and still relatively expensive compared to the DVD post-and-return services offered by companies such as LoveFilm.com (UK) and Netflix.com (US). That said, it is very convenient.

> **TIP:** When buying DVDs, keep an eye out for promotional codes that entitle you to a free iTunes digital version of the same movie that you have purchased on disc. This feature is becoming quite common and saves you the bother of ripping (see p.85) the film yourself to use on an iPod.

iTunes Wi-Fi Music Store

With an iPod touch, you can access the iTunes Store directly when connected to a Wi-Fi network (see p.212). Anything you download with be copied back to iTunes next time you sync. To get started, tap the iTunes icon on the Home screen and start browsing. Once you're looking at a list of tracks, you can:

▶**Tap a track's name** to hear a thirty-second preview.

▶**Tap a track's price** and then Buy Now to sign in to your store account and make a purchase.

If it's Apps that you want to download from the store, then turn to p.119.

More in the Store

Publish an iMix

As well as selling music, the iTunes Store gives you the option of publishing your own playlists so that others can either draw inspiration from (or snigger at) your impeccable taste. Note, though, that only songs available in the iTunes Store will be listed.

To publish a playlist, select it and choose Create an iMix… from the Store menu, or click the arrow next to its icon. To email a friend with the link to your published mix, click the arrow button next to the playlist and choose Tell a Friend.

Giving music

You can buy and send "Gift Certificates" as well as prepaid "iTunes Music Cards" that can be redeemed in the Store. The link is on the homepage with full instructions. Here you'll also see a link for setting up a "Monthly Gift" allowance account: you authorize someone to spend a set amount of money each month that is then charged to your credit card.

Billboard charts

The US iTunes Store also has a link on the homepage to the *Billboard* charts, and not just their current listing, but hit parades from years gone by. European shoppers can browse in the US Store via the dropdown menu on the homepage.

iTunes U

iTunes U ("university") makes available lectures, debates and presentations from US colleges as audio and video files. The service is free and has made unlikely stars of some of the more entertaining professors, Dutch physics lecturer Walter Lewin being one of the most popular. Look for the link on the Store's home page.

Freebies

Keep an eye open for free tracks: you get something for nothing, and you might discover an artist you never knew you liked. Also on offer are free-to-stream music videos, though you'll need a fast Internet connection to make them worth watching.

Click-wheel iPod Games

Click-wheel iPods come with a few basic built-in games. Buried within the Extras menu you'll find a couple of lo-fi staples, but you may want to check out the iPod Games section of the iTunes Store for something else. To get started, click the iPod Games link in the left-hand panel. Though there's nothing to compare to the gaming experience of the iPod touch (see p.119), the selection on offer is worth a look. Once downloaded, games are easily synced over to the iPod via the Games tab of your iPod's Options panel in iTunes.

10

Other download sources

The non-Apple options

Though it's the obvious choice for iTunes users, the iTunes Store doesn't hold all the cards when it comes to selling music and video online. There are many other legal download services out there – some of them are less expensive than iTunes and others offer tracks that iTunes doesn't. But while the iTunes Store may have competition from other commercial download services, it's probably fair to say that its primary competitor is P2P file sharing and other illegal methods of distributing music online. This chapter will bring you up to speed on both the best legal sites and services, and the not-so-legal ones that continue to fuel the dabate.

Legal downloads

You can't simply download a song from any website or service and assume it will play back in iTunes and on your Pod. Whether it will work depends on the type of file format the tracks are saved in, and whether or not the tracks have embedded DRM protection (see p.18).

Unfortunately for iPod owners, the majority of the big online music services (aside from the iTunes Store) offer DRM-protected WMA files. Currently, these won't play back in iTunes or on an iPod – at least not without some effort (see the tip on p.155). And this situation looks unlikely to change any time soon, since Apple are keen to keep people shopping at the iTunes Store rather than at any of its competitors.

Realistically, then, for legal music downloads, you're better off sticking with iTunes or the various services that offer unprotected MP3 files. Following is an alphabetical summary of the main legal music sites and services. Nearly all of these services are compatible with any MP3 player hardware or jukebox, but there are a few with specific quirks or limitations, so read the small print carefully before signing up.

Video download services

Watching streamed video online is commonplace thanks to YouTube and the growth of TV-on-demand websites. At the time of writing, however, there are no real alternatives to the iTunes Store when it comes to downloading movies or TV shows for use with iTunes and iPods. Amazon's Unbox download service, for example, only works on a PC and with Creative Zen portable players. Many people download video for free from P2P networks and BitTorrent sites (see p.113), but this isn't legal in the case of copyrighted movies and TV shows.

Whatever you download, you may need to convert it before it will play in iTunes or on an iPod. See p.83 for more information.

Russian MP3 sites

In between the legit and the illegit, there are MP3 websites that are, well, kind of legal. MP3million, for example, is the latest of a string of Russian sites that use a loophole in their country's broadcast law to openly offer a huge download archive without permission from the labels. It's left up to you to ensure you don't break the law of your own country when downloading. Other sites that have come and gone and that operate in the same way include ALLOFMP3.com and MP3Sparks.com.

MP3million mp3million.com

Amazon amazon.com
Launched in 2007, Amazon was the first store to offer exclusively DRM-free music in the MP3 format. There are millions of tracks, all of which can be downloaded directly to your iTunes or Windows Media library.

AudioLunchbox audiolunchbox.com
A top-class selection from independent labels. Most tracks are 99¢, though there are freebies to be had, too.

Bleep bleep.com
Electronica and indie, including everything from the Warp Records catalogue and loads more. You can preview whole tracks before buying, at which point expect to pay 99p per song or £6.99 for an album.

Download.com Music music.download.com
Free music by amateur or up-and-coming artists. It's the archive that used to live at MP3.com – now a site that lets you compare (and search for tracks across) the major music services.

eMusic emusic.com
Aside from Amazon, perhaps the main competitor to iTunes, this brilliant service offers 4 million songs from indie labels. For the $9.99 per month basic package you get 30 tracks – which works out at only 33¢ per track.

More music online: Last.fm and Spotify

Last.fm is an amazing free way to discover and listen to (and watch) new music – so good, in fact, that more than thirty million people have signed up. When you set up an account, Last.fm starts to keep track of what you listen to in iTunes and on your iPod – including your listening history. This information is analyzed – "Scrobbled" – and Last.fm starts to serve up custom streams of tracks based on your taste. The end result falls somewhere between being your own personal radio station and the iTunes Genius feature (see p.134). Spotify, meanwhile, lets you stream content from an online archive in a similar way, this time via a downloadable application. In exchange for the privilege, you can either put up with occasional servings of audio advertising, or, for a monthly fee, go ad-free. Though neither service results in an offline music collection, you do benefit from an always-on stream of music that you like.

Last.fm last.fm
Spotify spotify.com

IntoMusic intomusic.co.uk
Indie and alternative stuff for 60p per track. There are subscription and buy-in-bulk payment options for keen users.

Mondomix mp3.mondomix.com
A one-stop shop for World Music MP3s from around the globe.

MySpace.com music.myspace.com
Literally tens-of-thousands of bands and artists representing every genre of music under the sun. Most offer, at the very least, a few songs to be streamed from their page, while others make their tracks available as either free or pay-for MP3 downloads.

Napster napster.co.uk (UK) napster.com (US)
Having inherited its name from the renowned illegal music sharing system that was shut down in 2002, the current Napster service offers "permanent" downloads at 99¢/79p per song or unlimited access to millions of tracks in return for a monthly fee. Napster does not officially work with iTunes, iPods or Macs. But PC users might be interested to check out the service, perhaps even to use alongside iTunes.

Supermarket sites

The supermarket chains are doing their best to take a slice of the music download market. While they may not carry the millions of tracks found on iTunes, both Tesco in the UK and Walmart in the US offer among the most competitive prices for mainstream artist selections.

Tesco tescodigital.com
Walmart mp3.walmart.com

Rhapsody real.com/rhapsody
Unlimited access to more than three million songs for $13 per month (computer only) or $15 per month (if you want to use an MP3 player). "Permanent" downloads are separate, at 79–99¢ per track. This service is available for both Mac and PC users, but not outside the US.

Illegal downloads

Collectively, all the commercial online music services described in the previous section, along with iTunes, are competing with P2P file sharing, a technology that allows computer users all over the world to "share" each other's files – including music files – via the Internet. Even if you've never heard of P2P ("peer-to-peer") you've probably heard of some of the programs that have made this kind of file sharing possible, such as KaZaA and, historically speaking, Napster. And you've probably also heard people debating the legal and moral ins and outs of the free-for-all that file-sharing programs facilitate.

The legal battle

Continuous legal action saw Napster – the first major P2P system – bludgeoned into submission (it has now resurfaced as one of the larger legitimate online music providers; see opposite). A similar

A peer-to-peer primer

On a home or office network, it's standard for users of each computer to have some degree of access to the files stored on the other computers. P2P file-sharing programs apply this idea to the whole of the Internet – which is, of course, simply a giant network of computers. In short, anyone who installs a P2P program can access the "shared folder" of anyone else running a similar program. And these shared folders are mostly filled with music and video files.

With literally millions of file sharers online at any one time, an unthinkably large quantity of content is up there. And it's not just music and video: any file can be made available, from images to software and documents. So, whether you're after a drum'n'bass track, a Web-design application, a Chomsky speech or an episode of *Friends*, you're almost certain to find it. But that doesn't mean that it's legal. If you download or make available any copyright-protected material, you are breaking the law and, while it's still currently unlikely, in theory, you could be prosecuted.

fate befell Scour, this time because of movie rather than audio sharing. But these casualties just paved the way for the many alternatives, of which the most popular has proved to be KaZaA, which now stands by some margin as the most downloaded program in the history of the Internet.

The music, film and software companies continued to fight back. In 2005, the Recording Industry Association of America (RIAA) and the Motion Picture Industry (MPI) were successful in closing down the company behind the Grokster P2P program.

In the meantime, the music industry, led by RIAA, has focused on people who clearly *are* breaking the law: individual file sharers downloading or making available copyrighted material. Quite a few individuals have now been prosecuted, but with many millions of people using file sharing each day, it seems very unlikely that the record companies could go after every one of them.

Whether or not it's ethical to use P2P to download copyrighted material for free is another question. Some people justify it on the grounds that they use file sharing as a way to listen to new music

iP2P?

The market position of iTunes and the iPod is often said to be strengthened by the wide range of third-party software and accessories available for it. But among these are programs that must make Apple – who are eager to get on the right side of the music industry – cringe. It was only a matter of time, for example, before someone developed a program to turn the Mac version of iTunes into a file-sharing program, allowing users around the globe to browse and download from the libraries of others. That program was iCommune (*icommune.net*), though legal wranglings stopped it taking the Net by storm.

they're considering buying on CD; others claim they refuse to support a music industry that, in their view, is doing more harm than good; others still only download non-controversial material, such as recordings of speeches, or music that they already own on CD or vinyl and can't be bothered to rip or record manually.

It's a heated debate – as is the question of whether file sharing has damaged legal music sales, something the industry insists upon, but which many experts claim is questionable.

Networks and programs

Though all P2P file sharing takes place via the Internet, there are various discrete "networks", the main ones being BitTorrent, eDonkey2000, FastTrack and Gnutella. Each is huge and accessible via various different programs, many of which are very sophisticated, with built-in media players or even the ability to import downloaded tracks directly into a playlist in iTunes.

Note that some file-sharing programs come with unwelcome extras such as spyware and adware – something long associated with KaZaA, for example. So proceed with care.

Below is a list of major networks and some of the most popular programs for accessing them. All of these can be downloaded and used for free, though some nag users to make a donation to the developer or pay for a more fully featured, ad-free version. Note that new P2P programs come out all the time and some programs can access more than one network.

Gnutella

Gnutella is a very popular network accessible via a wide range of user-friendly programs such as:

LimeWire limewire.com (PC & Mac)
Morpheus morpheus.com (PC)
Acquisition acquisitionx.com (Mac)
Shareaza sourceforge.net/projects/shareaza (PC)

FastTrack

Thanks to the success of KaZaA, this extremely well-stocked network has been the focus of much of the legal battle. Applications for accessing the network include:

KaZaA kazaa.com (PC)
Poisoned gottsilla.net (Mac)

Since 2004, iMesh has offered a legal option for accessing the FastTrack network from the US and Canada. Now recognized by the record labels' association, the site charges a monthly subscription fee to tap into the shared library of millions of songs.

iMesh imesh.com (PC)

And more...

There are many other programs and networks out there. SoulSeek, for example, is popular for underground and alternative music, and allows users to download whole folders at once.

SoulSeek slsknet.org (PC & Mac)
SolarSeek solarseek.net (Mac)

BitTorrent

With most P2P systems, users search for the files they are after within the P2P program itself and then download them directly to other users. An exception to this rule is BitTorrent. WIth this system, users first search the Web for so-called torrent files of the music or video they're after. These small files are quickly downloaded and opened with a BitTorrent application, which then downloads – or at least tries to download – the music or video from a variety of other users. The more people who are using a particular torrent, the faster the data flows and the quicker each person's download arrives.

BitTorrent is hugely popular for large files – especially albums, movies and television shows. Indeed, according to some estimates, it sometimes accounts for as much as a quarter of Internet traffic. As with the other networks, however, using torrents to download copyrighted material is against the law.

To get started with BitTorrent, you first have to download a suitable application (or "client"). There are numerous options out there, including several of the P2P programs listed in this chapter. But the most popular dedicated torrent clients are BitTorrent and Vuze. The latter is particularly slick and, as well as the inevitable contraband, offers access to an extensive network of non-copyrighted material, including hundreds of intriguing if not necessarily entertaining "fan-made" sci-fi movies.

BitTorrent bittorrent.com
Vuze vuze.com (PC & Mac)

For more information, including reviews of all the available programs, see:

Slyck slyck.com (PC & Mac)
ZeroPaid zeropaid.com (PC & Mac)

11

Podcasts & radio

Tuning in online

Traditionally, online radio has worked pretty much like radio in the real world, except that the choice of stations is almost endless. You're limited neither by your geographical area nor your next-door neighbour's four-storey gazebo. This is great for listening on your computer, but it can be a hassle, and legally dodgy, to get traditional "streamed" online radio shows onto an iPod. Hence the recent emergence of podcasts – a new type of online radio aimed specifically at the MP3-player generation. And it's a craze that iTunes has endeavoured to make very much its own. Podcasts are produced by everyone from the BBC to wannabe pundits operating out of their bedrooms. They're easy to make and even easier to find and download.

Podcasts

Unlike most online radio, which is "streamed" across the Net in real time, podcasts are made available as audio files that can be downloaded and played on your computer or iPod. Podcasts are usually free and often consist of spoken content, and sometimes music too, though there's a grey area surrounding the distribution of copyrighted music in this way.

Most podcasts are audio-only, but there are also a huge number of video podcasts available, ranging from the comedic (*The Ricky Gervais Podcast*) to the didactic (*Learn Excel with MrExcel*).

Subscribing to podcasts

It's often possible to download a single podcast "show" directly from the website of whoever produced it, but it's far easier to use iTunes to subscribe to each of the podcasts you're interested in.

Open iTunes and click Podcasts in the Sources sidebar. Next, click the Podcast Directory link (at the bottom) and browse or search for interesting-looking podcasts. When you find one that looks up your street, click subscribe and iTunes will automatically download the most recent episode to your iTunes Library, ready for transfer to your iPod. (Depending on the podcast, you may also be offered all the previous episodes to download.)

To change how iTunes handles podcasts, look under the relevant tab in iTunes Preferences. For example, if disk space is at a premium on your system, tell iTunes to delete older episodes after a week or so.

> **TIP:** If you don't get on with iTunes, or you want to get hold of podcasts for a non-iPod MP3 player, try a third-party aggregator such as iPodder (ipodder. sourceforge.net) or Jax (joesoft.com).

Creating your own podcast

Once you've subscribed and listened to a few podcasts you might decide it's time to turn your hand to broadcasting and get in on the action. Without going into too much detail, this is how it's done via the iTunes Store.

▶ **Record your episode** This can be done pretty easily using a microphone and any of the programs we mention on p.73. When you're finished, save the episode in MP3 or AAC format.

▶ **Create an RSS feed** This is a bit fiddly, but you'll soon get the hang of it. You need nothing more than a text editor, which you'll already have in the form of Notepad (PC) or TextEdit (Mac). For full details read the tutorial at apple.com/itunes/podcasts/techspecs.html

> **TIP:** iTunes podcasting supports various audio (.m4a, .mp3) and video (.mov, .mp4, .m4v) file formats and even .pdf document files. Using a program such as GarageBand (see p.73), you can create AAC (.m4a) files that include chapter divisions as well as images that will show up as "album artwork" in both iTunes and on an iPod.

▶ **Upload your podcast** Find or hire some Web space (most Internet connection accounts offer a bit for free), and use an FTP program to upload both the RSS feed and your audio files.

RSS

RSS (Really Simple Syndication) is the technology behind regular blogs as well as podcasts (which are basically audio blogs). When you subscribe to a podcast, your aggregator program (iTunes for example) hooks up with an RSS file, also known as an RSS feed, which is stored online. This file contains information about all the episodes of the podcast and points iTunes to the relevant sound files. The RSS feed is written in a relatively simple code called XML (it's a bit like the HTML of regular webpages), which makes it quite easy to do yourself (see above).

Your receipt

Danbury Public Library
170 Main Street
Danbury, CT 06810

TO RENEW:
Visit danburylibrary.org
or CALL (203) 797-4505

Customer Name: GALLAGHER, MARK

Items that you checked out

Title: iPod & iTunes for dummies / by Tony
Bove
ID: 34008068131807
Due: **Friday, February 14, 2020**

Title: The rough guide to iPods & iTunes /
Peter Buckley
ID: 34008067847833
Due: **Friday, February 14, 2020**

Total items: 2
Account balance: $0.10
/24/2020 2:28 PM
Checked out: 2
Overdue: 0
Ready for pickup: 0

Thank you for using the bibliotheca SelfCheck
System.

▶**Test your feed** Open iTunes. Choose Subscribe to Podcast... from the Advanced menu and enter the URL (online address) of your RSS feed file. If your podcast downloads, you know it's working fine.

▶ **Submit your podcast to iTunes** From iTunes click the iTunes Store link in the Sources sidebar, then find your way to the store's Podcasts page and click the big "Submit a Podcast" button.

Internet radio

Radio in iTunes

Radio in iTunes is extremely simple. Connect to the Internet, click the Radio icon in the Sources sidebar and browse through the list of genres and stations. For each station you'll see a bitrate – this is important as you will only enjoy a glitch-free listening experience if you select stations which stream at a bitrate that is slower than your Internet connection.

When you've found a station you like the look of, double-click it, wait a few seconds, and the stream should begin. You can create shortcuts to your favourites by dragging them into a playlist.

> **TIP:** If your iTunes radio is prone to glitches, try increasing the Streaming Buffer Size to Large under the Advanced tab in iTunes Preferences.

More Internet radio...

iTunes only scratches the surface of Internet radio. Search Google or browse a directory such as radio.about.com, and you'll find thousands more stations. Most are accessed via a website. All you need to tune in, if you don't have them already, are the right media players: RealPlayer (there's a free version buried in the site) and

Windows Media Player (also free, available for Mac and PC).

RealPlayer real.com
Windows Media Player windowsmedia.com/download

> **TIP:** If you are a Mac user and want to shoehorn BBC radio streams into iTunes, download the third-party script found at: cultofmac.com/bbc-radio-in-itunes

...and onto the iPod

There are two main limitations with online radio. One is that, though some online radio stations offer programmes "on demand", you generally have to be in the right place at the right time to listen to them. Second, you can't access online radio with a click-wheel iPod. However, there are programs available specifically for getting around these limitations by recording radio onto your hard drive as MP3 files. But be aware that, depending on your country and the station, recording from a radio stream may not be strictly legal.

HiDownload hidownload.com (PC)
RadioLover bitcartel.com/radiolover (Mac)

iPod touch owners can also search the App Store (see Chapter 12, opposite) for third-party tools for accessing Internet radio over Wi-Fi networks.

iPod FM Radio Remote

You can also listen to radio on an iPod the old-fashioned way. Apple's Radio Remote accessory, available for $50/£35 connects to your Pod via the Dock connector socket (so it won't work with a shuffle) and tunes into FM radio. Once attached, you can control the radio either using the standard iPod controls or with the little remote unit halfway up the earphone cable.

12

The App Store

Limitless possibilities…

Straight out of the box, the iPod touch is a feature-heavy device compared to other iPods, but that really is just the start of the story. In terms of functionality, the sky's the limit, thanks to downloadable applications, or "apps", available from Apple's App Store – part of the iTunes Store. It all kicked off in the spring of 2008, when Apple made available the tools that developers needed to start building "proper" applications that could be installed on the iPhone and touch. The developer community was swift to sign up to this new "open" platform and there are now countless apps available. To date, more than one billion apps have been downloaded. It is beyond the scope of this book to explore every app (as there are literally thousands), so, instead, here's a brief overview of how the App Store works along with a few of our favourites to get you started.

Downloading apps

The App Store offers everything from free utilities to fully fledged versions of computer games, which, as you might expect, will cost you a few bucks (payable through your regular iTunes account, see p.99). The App Store can be accessed in two ways:

▶ **On the iPod touch** The App Store on the iPod touch looks and works in exactly the same way as the iTunes Store – there's a "Featured" section, a search box, and various categories to browse. Obviously, you'll need a Wi-Fi connection to actually get in there to start browsing and downloading the goods.

▶ **On a Mac or PC** In iTunes, open the iTunes Store and click through to the App Store department. Anything you download will be synced across to your iPod touch next time you connect.

Managing apps

Just like with music and video files, iTunes allows you to be selective about which of your apps are synced across to your iPod at any one time. Connect your Pod to iTunes, and then make your selections by checking the boxes under the Apps tab of the iPod Options panel.

Updating apps

One of the best features of the App Store is that as and when developers release updates for their software, you will automatically be informed of the update and given the option to install it for free, even if you had to shell out for the original download.

On the touch, choose App Store > Updates to download newer versions of your apps. The Updates icon displays a numbered red circle to let you know how many apps are available and those that you grab are then synced back to iTunes next time you connect.

This is all well and good, but it is far easier done through iTunes. Highlight Applications in the Sources sidebar to view all your apps and then click the Check for updates button, bottom-right, to see what's new.

Deleting apps

It's worth noting that your iTunes account keeps a permanent record of which apps you have downloaded, so if you do happen to delete both your Pod's copy and the iTunes copy, you can go back to the store and download it again at no extra charge. Here's how to delete an app:

▶ **On the iPod touch** Hold down any Home screen icon until they all start jiggling around and then tap the small red ⊗ on the corner of the app you want to delete. When you have finished, hit the Pod's Home button.

▶ **On a Mac or PC** Highlight Applications in the Sources sidebar and then right-click the unwanted app and choose Delete from the menu that appears.

What's available?

Every conceivable type of software is available in the App Store, but be aware that many apps may well only be suited to iPhones, and not the touch, so always check the stated "Requirements" of an app before you download it. Here are a few popular examples to give you a sense of what's up there:

▶ **Skype (free)** With this app, a Skype account, and some earphones with a built-in mic (see p.131), you can make phone calls over Wi-Fi networks. You can also receive Skype calls, assuming the app is running on the iPod at the time.

▶ **eBay (free)** This app from eBay's own stable offers all the tools you need to keep track of your buying and selling activity.

▶ **TypePad (free)** One of the leading photo and text blogging tools comes to the iPod.

▶ **Otis (99¢/59p)** Beautifully rendered block strategy game … very frustrating … addictive.

▶ **Bloom ($3.99/£2.39)** Designed by Brian Eno, this app lets you create your own ambient music with accompanying hypnotic visuals.

▶ **PocketGuitar (99¢/59p)** More music … this time a strummable, customizable guitar, complete with fret board.

▶ **Remember The Milk (free)** By far the best To Do list manager in the App Store.

▶ **iHusky Lite (free)** Now you can tickle a virtual puppy whenever you want.

> **TIP:** Once installed on the iPod, many apps install their very own options panel at the bottom of the regular list of settings behind the Settings icon on the Home screen.

Organizing
& playing

13

Browsing & playing in iTunes

Look and listen...

Most people who use iTunes barely scratch the surface of what the application is capable of, opting to accept the iTunes environment in its virgin state. This chapter explains how to make the most of the browsing, searching and playing tools at your fingertips – from customizing columns and the Genius feature, to the Browser and multiple windows.

Searching

The Search box, on the right-hand side at the top of the iTunes environment, lets you find a track by typing all or part of the name of the artist, album, track title or composer. You can search more than one field at once, so typing *Bee Vio*, for example, would bring up Beethoven's violin concerto.

Note that iTunes will only search those tracks currently in the Song List. So if you want to search your whole music collection, make sure the Music icon is selected in the Sources sidebar, and "All" is selected in the Genre column of the iTunes Browser (if you are using it) before you start to type. Equally, if you only want to search through your movies, make sure that Movies is selected in the Sources sidebar before you search.

> **TIP:** If you ever come to iTunes and great swathes of your collection seem to have vanished, check whether anything has been typed into the Search field, as this may be the reason for the incomplete listings.

Browsing

One of the best additions to iTunes in recent years were the three view modes, accessible via the View menu or using the set of buttons next to the Search box. They are:

List View

List View presents your music, video, podcasts and so on as a sortable list with many columns. You can sort the list by any column by clicking on the header of that column. Click a second time and the order is reversed (with the small black triangle on the header flipping to indicate the direction of the ordering). You can jump to a particular point in the list by pressing a letter or number: if you sort by artist and press "R", say, you might jump to The Rolling Stones.

In addition, you can add and remove many other columns. To do this, either summon the View Options box from the Edit menu or use the keyboard shortcuts ⌘J (Mac) or Ctrl-J (PC). Alternatively, try right-clicking the header of any of the columns in the main iTunes pane to reveal a dropdown menu of columns, as pictured above.

Once you've checked all the columns you want to see, and unchecked those you don't, contents of the main iTunes pane should change to reflect this. But that's not all. You can also adjust

TIP: Double-clicking a divider between two column headers will Auto Size the left-hand column, changing its width to ensure that everything in it is visible.

the relative width of the columns, by dragging the dividing lines between the headers, and also rearrange them, by dragging their headers left or right.

Note that when you customize the List View in these ways, your changes will only apply to whichever item is currently highlighted in the Sources sidebar. This is handy, since different playlists require different columns. For a dance selection, you might want to view the Beats Per Minute column, say, while a classical playlist would obviously need the Composer column.

The Browser

The "Browser" (a panel above the main song list, with columns for artist, album and genre) is a very important feature of List View, allowing you to browse quickly and easily. The Browser appears by default when you switch to List View and can be hidden by dragging the strip just below it upwards. To bring it back into view select Show Browser from the View menu, or hit ⌘B (Mac) or Ctrl-B (PC) on your keyboard.

Clicking an entry under Genre reveals the artists from that genre; clicking an entry under Artists, in turn, reveals all the albums of that artist. And, with each selection, the list below changes to display only the relevant songs.

> **TIP:** You can edit track info from Browser entries, which is handy for quickly changing all "Beatles" tracks, say, to "The Beatles". Simply select a genre, artist or album and choose Get Info from the File menu.

Grid View

Grid View works similarly to parts of the iTunes Store. The contents of your library is displayed against a black background with all tracks bound together by either album, artist, composer or genre, depending which button you select at the top of the panel. Try right-clicking these buttons to reveal additional sorting options, and scaling the grid using the slider to the right. Each of the four Grid View alternatives comes into its own in a different way:

▶ **Albums** Great for quickly trawling through your collection to look for missing artwork and inconsistent album labelling.

▶ **Artists** Again, a nice visual way to look for inconsistent labelling. You can also select which album cover is used to represent an artist. Drag across the artist's image to view alternatives, and when you see the one you want, right-click and choose "Set Default Grid Artwork".

▶ **Genres** iTunes supplies its own default artwork for many common genres; alternatively, you can choose your own, as above.

▶ **Composers** Really useful if you listen to a lot of classical music; but be careful, unless your iTunes library labelling is fastidious, the results can seem a little eccentric.

Cover Flow View

Cover Flow is a superb feature, allowing you to flick through your music collection by album artwork. It's like rummaging through an old stack of LPs, or browsing in a record store.

Cover Flow started out life as a third-party tool created by programmer Jonathan del Strother; iTunes users could download it as an alternative way to browse their music. Apple liked it so much they incorporated it first into iTunes, then into the iPhone, and finally into the iPod.

Once in Cover Flow mode, browse using the on-screen scroll bar or the left and right arrows on the keyboard. Tap Enter or double-click a cover to start playing.

> **TIP:** You can put Cover Flow into full-screen mode, either by clicking the icon to the right of the scroll bar or using the shortcut ⌘F (Mac) and Ctrl-F (PC).

FluidTunes

If you like Cover Flow, you'll be intrigued by FluidTunes (fluidtunes.com). Though not really practical on a day-to-day basis, this third-party download lets you control iTunes on a Mac by waving at it via your computer's iSight camera. If nothing else, it's a great ice-breaker at parties. It's free to download and try.

Play modes

In its default state, iTunes will play whichever tracks are currently displayed, in the order shown, and then stop. But there are various other options…

Repeat

iTunes offers two repeat modes, which are available via the Controls menu or the button on the bottom-left of the iTunes window. Repeat All plays whatever is currently displayed round and round forever. Repeat One repeats just the current track.

> **TIP:** On a click-wheel iPod, you can toggle the various Shuffle and Repeat modes within the Settings menu. On an iPod touch, tap the album artwork of the currently playing track and look for the repeat ⇆ and shuffle ⤬ mode icons, which work in the same way as the iTunes buttons described above and below.

Shuffle

When Shuffle is turned on, iTunes plays back the currently displayed tracks in random order – though random isn't necessarily the right word (see box overleaf). Again, this function can be toggled on and off in the Controls menu or using the Shuffle button at the bottom-left of the iTunes window.

> **TIP:** If you're using Shuffle and you want to see what's coming next, click the top of the track-number column. If you don't like the order iTunes has selected, reshuffle by turning Shuffle mode off and back on, or by holding down Alt (Mac) or Shift (PC) and clicking the Shuffle button.

How random is Shuffle?

Though there's no such thing as true random-order generation, computers can do an excellent job of simulating genuine disorder. But ever since the early days of iTunes and iPods, users have complained of a distinct presence of pattern, even predictability, in the "random" selections generated by the Shuffle mode. Perhaps it's just superstition – no one outside Apple HQ seems to know how Shuffle actually works – but people claim to hear certain artists or tunes appearing more than others, and genres or artists appearing in chunks.

iTunes 5 improved things with the introduction of Smart Shuffle, which let you choose from a sliding scale of randomness, from "more likely" to "less likely" (expect decidedly odd juxtapositions). However, in one of their own seemingly inexplicably random moments, Apple pulled the feature. So, once again, Shuffle is hard-wired in "less likely" mode.

You can, however, choose to have your Shuffle mode proceed by whole albums or groupings instead of individual songs. You'll find this option in iTunes Preferences, under Playback, and also in the Controls menu.

If you want to add to your long-term randomness, try ensuring that Shuffle mode doesn't return to one track until it has played all the others, even between multiple listening sessions. To do this, create a Smart Playlist (see p.141) for songs which have a Play Count of less than, say, two. When the music finally stops, change the Play Count setting to 3. And so on…

One final Shuffle tip: if you don't want a specific track to appear in any Shuffle selections, highlight the track, press Get Info in the File menu and, under Options, select "Skip when shuffling".

iTunes DJ

iTunes DJ, found in the Sources sidebar, is a play mode that generates a random mix of tracks drawn from either a playlist of your choice or your entire Library. When iTunes DJ is being used, a new panel appears at the bottom of the main iTunes pane; here you can regenerate the track list automatically, by hitting the Refresh button, and you can also move specific tracks to the top of the list by right-clicking them and selecting "Play next in iTunes DJ". But the really fun thing about iTunes DJ is the way it uses "Votes" to move tracks up the order of play. To start using votes, click the Settings button and check the Enable Voting box. There

Take a moment to look at all the iTunes DJ options on offer behind the Settings button before allowing guests to vote using the Remote app.

are a few ways votes can be added. They are, in brief:

▶ **Right-click** any song in your Library, another playlist (or even in the iTunes DJ list) and choose "Add to iTunes DJ". Repeat this multiple times to add extra votes.

▶ **Drag** any selections from anywhere in your Library onto the iTunes DJ icon in the Sources sidebar.

▶**Via Apple's Remote app** Available as a free download (see p.241 for more), Remote can be used to place votes (simply tap the heart icons to vote) from either an iPhone or iPod touch on the same Wi-Fi network as the Mac or PC hosting the iTunes DJ list. Remote users can also browse the source of the DJ list and request that other songs be added.

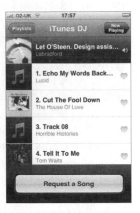

If you don't want to see the iTunes DJ icon in the Sources sidebar, you can choose to hide it by unchecking the box under the General settings in iTunes Preferences.

Genius

Like both Shuffle
and iTunes DJ,
the iTunes Genius
feature takes the
responsibility of
what to play out of
your hands. This
time around, the
list is not randomly selected, however, but is instead based to a
large degree upon accumulated iTunes Store information. In short,
the Genius algorithms recognize that, for example, people who
like The Beatles may well also like The Rolling Stones. In Apple's
own words, it selects songs "that go great together".

To start, select any song in your library that matches your mood
and either right-click to select Start Genius or click the ✤ button
found at the bottom of the iTunes frame.

Updating Genius data

For Genius to work well it will from time to time go online to
cross-reference your library against an iTunes Store database of
Genius recommendations. You can also manually update your
Genius data by choosing Store > Genius.

Genius Sidebar

Next to the ✤ button in iTunes is the ◀ button, which toggles the
Genius Sidebar on and off. It's best kept hidden for everyday use,
as it does little more than recommend music in the iTunes Store
based on what you are listening to – there's enough advertising in
the world without iTunes trying it on too.

> **TIP:** To find out how to use the Genius feature on
> your iPod, turn to p.51 and p.54.

Visualizer

If you are not content just to sit and watch a small dot plodding its way across the iTunes status area, turn on Visualizer from the View menu. It's a psychedelic light show that swirls and morphs in time with the music. Depending on your taste, it will either hypnotize you into a state of blissful paralysis or – more likely – annoy the hell out of you.

To be fair, the default Visualizer is impressive compared to the "Classic" version found in older iTunes incarnations (it's now buried in a sub-menu if you want to take a look).

> **TIP:** Visualizer can also be turned on using the shortcut ⌘T (Mac) and Ctrl-T (PC). To toggle full-screen mode on and off use ⌘F (Mac) and Ctrl-F (PC).

Visualizer plug-ins

If you get bored of the built-in iTunes visuals you can always add more. There are loads to be found online, at sites such as:

Arkaos arkaos.net
JCode jcode.org
PluginsWorld.com pluginsworld.com

Once you've downloaded some plug-ins, install them by dragging them to the iTunes Plug-ins folder. You'll find this folder on a Mac within your home folder, under Library > iTunes. On a PC, it's within the iTunes folder inside My Music.

Managing iTunes windows

As with any other program, iTunes windows can be re-sized by dragging the bottom-right corner, and also minimized – hidden from view but still active and accessible via the Dock (on a Mac) or Taskbar (on a PC). This is done in the normal way:

on a Mac, click the small yellow button in the top-left corner of the window, or press ⌘M; on a PC, click the minimize button on the window's top-right corner (pictured), or press M while holding down the Windows key.

Multiple windows

When managing and arranging your music, don't feel obliged to keep everything confined to a single iTunes window: double-clicking a highlighted item in the Sources sidebar will open its contents in a new floating frame.

This is all standard stuff but, unlike most other programs, iTunes also provides a halfway house between a window being open and minimized: a miniaturized version offering access to essential player controls and, if desired, the status display. This "MiniPlayer" is great if you want to keep an eye on what's playing, skip tracks you don't like and so on, while working in another program. To launch the MiniPlayer, click the small green button in the top left of the window (Mac) or use the keyboard shortcuts Ctrl-⌘Z (Mac) or Ctrl-M (PC). The mini player that pops up can be further shrunk by dragging its corner.

> **TIP:** If you want the MiniPlayer to sit on top of other open windows and applications – handy if you want to skip a song, say, while surfing the Web – check the option under the Advanced tab of iTunes Preferences.

Playing tips

▶**When a song is playing but you've browsed elsewhere**, use the SnapBack arrow in the right of the Status area to show the currently playing song.

▶ **If a song is too quiet**, select it, click Get Info in the File menu, and under Options boost its level using the Volume Adjustment slider. You can also do this for multiple songs at once.

▶ **iTunes can "bookmark" tracks**, remembering where you'd got to so that, if you skip to another track halfway through (or switch

iTunes off completely), it will return to where you left off next time
you play the track in question. This is especially useful for audiobooks.
To switch this feature on, select a track, choose Get Info from the File
menu and check "Remember playback position" under Options.

▶ **If you want songs to melt into each other seamlessly**,
open Preferences and, under Playback, mess around with the
"Crossfade playback" settings.

▶**The Space bar**, on your computer keyboard, offers a quick and
easy way to pause and resume playback of music and video in iTunes.

▶ **Playing videos** When you play a video
it fills the whole of the iTunes Window. Move
the mouse over the frame to reveal player and
scubber controls. Click the ▦ icon to enter
full-screen mode and the ⊗ icon, top-left, to
quit the movie and return to your iTunes library.

▶ **Dock controls** On a Mac you can access
a menu of the most useful iTunes controls by
clicking and holding the mouse over the iTunes
icon on the OS X Dock. The PC version offers
something similar via the iTunes icon in the
System Tray (by the clock).

TIP: Mac-users who would like to access iTunes
controls from the OS X menu bar should
investigate a third-party application called "You Control iTunes",
free to download from yousoftware.com/tunes.

14

Playlists
The new mix tape

A key feature of any computer jukebox software is the ability to create playlists: homemade combinations of tracks for playing on your computer or iPod; for burning to CD; for sending to friends; or even for publishing online. Like the old-fashioned mix tape, a playlist can be made for a particular time, place or person, or just for fun. Unlike with cassettes, however, playlists can be created instantly; they can  be as long as you like; they won't be poor sound quality; and there's no need to buy physical media.

The basics

The first thing to know about playlists is
that they don't actually contain any music.
All they contain is a list of pointers to tracks
within your collection. So you can delete
playlists, or individual tracks within them,
without deleting the actual music files.
Likewise, you can add the same track to as
many playlists as you like without using up
extra disk space.

Playlists appear in the Sources sidebar on
the left of the iTunes window. If iTunes came
with a few playlists when you installed it,
don't be afraid to delete them.

Creating playlists

To create a new playlist, either hit the new playlist
button (the **+**) at the bottom-left of the iTunes window, or use the keyboard shortcut: ⌘N for Macs, or
Ctrl-N for PCs. Either way, a new playlist icon will appear in the
Sources sidebar, highlighted and ready to be named and filled. You
can drag individual songs into the new list or – using the Browser
– add entire albums, artists or genres in one fell swoop.
You can also create a new playlist by dragging songs, artists,
albums or genres directly onto some blank space in the playlist
area, or by selecting a bunch of material and choosing New
playlist from the File menu.

> **TIP:** If an iPod is connected, selected and set to
> manual management (see p.45), clicking the new
> playlist button will create a new playlist directly on the iPod.

Rearranging, renaming and deleting playlists

When viewing the contents of a playlist in List View, you can sort its contents by any category by clicking the top of the relevant column. Or, to sort them manually, first sort by the number column and then drag the tracks at will.

To rename a playlist, click its name once and then again (not too fast). To delete one, highlight it and press the backspace key; select Clear from the Edit or right-click menus; or, on a Mac, drag the icon into the Trash.

> **TIP:** The currently viewed track order of a playlist is copied over to your iPod when you update. On the Pod you can't rearrange tracks, so make sure the playlists are sorted to your taste before updating.

Smart Playlists

Smart Playlists, rather than being compiled manually by you, are put together by iTunes according to a set of rules, or "conditions", that you define. It might be songs with a certain word in their title, or a set of genres, or the tracks you listened to the most – or a combination of any of these kinds of things.

The clever thing about Smart Playlists is that their contents will automatically change over time, as relevant tracks are added to your Library or existing tracks meet the criteria by being, say, rated highly.

To create a new Smart Playlist, look in the File menu or click the New Playlist button while holding down Alt (Mac) or Shift (PC) – you'll see the plus sign change into a cog. This will open the Smart Playlist box (as shown overleaf), where you set the parameters for the new list. Simply click **+** and **–** to add and remove rules. It's like a bizarre kind of musical algebra.

Use the ⊕
and ⊖ buttons
to add or
remove rules.

Use the dropdown
menus to choose
which kinds of rules
you want to apply.

To edit the rules of an existing Smart Playlist, select it and choose Edit Smart Playlist in the File menu – or in the menu you get by right-clicking.

Playlist folders

Once you've amassed scores of playlists, you may find it useful to keep them organized in folders. You'll find the option to create a folder within the File menu. Once you've created one, you can simply drag playlists – or even other folders – into it.

These playlist folders are in turn copied over onto iPods – very useful when drilling down through your music when out and about.

Smart Playlist ideas

Smart Playlists give you the opportunity to be creative with the way you organize the songs in your Library; they can be both a lot of fun and very useful. So much so, in fact, that there are whole websites devoted to the subject (such as *smartplaylists.com*).

Following are a few examples to give you an idea of the kinds of things you can do with Smart Playlist.

Functional...

Tracks I've never heard
▶ *Play Count is 0*
Lets you hear music that you've ripped or downloaded but not yet played.

On the up
▶ *Date Added is in the last 30 days*
▶ *My Rating is greater than 3 stars*
▶ *Play Count is less than 5*
A playlist of new songs that you like, but which deserve more of a listen.

The old Joanna
▶ *Grouping contains piano*
If you use Grouping or Comment fields (see p.148) to tag tracks by instrument, mood or anything else, you can then create Smart Playlists based on this info.

...or inspirational

A compilation of questions
▶ *Song Name contains "?"*
For days with no answers.

Space songs
▶ *Song Name contains "space"*
▶ *Song Name contains "stars"*
▶ *Song Name contains "moon"*
▶ *Song Name contains "rocket"*
For those who love their sci-fi as much as their music.

Create playlists on the iPod

If you're out and about and you want to set up a playlist there and then, you can do so with the iPod's On-The-Go playlist function. On a click-wheel iPod, browse your music and when you come across a song, artist, album or even a whole genre you'd like to add, press and hold the Select button. After around a second the selection's name will flash to let you know that it has been added to the On-The-Go playlist – which you'll find at the bottom of the Playlists menu. You can easily clear or save your On-The-Go playlist using the options you'll find within the list itself, below the tracks.

On an iPod touch the process is slightly different. Tap Music > Playlists and choose On-The-Go. The iPod then shows you a list of all your songs, which you can add to by tapping. Less obviously, you can also click any of the buttons at the bottom of the screen to browse by album, playlist, artist and so on, and add tracks from there. When you are finished compiling, tap Done. You can return to and change your new playlist at any time. Tap Playlists, then On-The-Go, and hit Edit.

> **TIP:** You can add to an On-The-Go playlist while it's playing. For example, you could add one track, set the playlist going, and then add more.

And finally...

So you've created a dream playlist, and it's just too good to keep all for yourself. What next? You could:

► **Burn it to CD** (see p.164)
► **Design the artwork** (see p.167)
► **Publish it as an iMix** (see p.103)

15

Tagging & tidying

iTunes housekeeping

Overlapping genres, unwanted tracks strewn all over the place, the same artist labelled in various different ways … use iTunes for a few months and you may find everything getting rather messy. This chapter tells you how to keep it all tidy and exploit the ways in which iTunes lets you assign different types of information to each song or video file. It also covers converting music from one format to another using the built-in tools found within iTunes.

Editing track info

Music and video files can include all sorts of information (known as metadata or tags) about their contents, from the artist and album names to tempo and sample rate. When you download or import a file, some of this info will usually be included. However, many details will be missing, and the data that is included may contain errors or clash with your preferred way of categorizing things. You might, for example, end up with an album by "Davis, Miles" when you'd prefer to use "Miles Davis".

Thankfully, existing track information can be easily edited, and extra data can be added. The more accurate and complete your tagging, the more flexibility you'll have when browsing or sorting your collection and creating Smart Playlists.

Editing info track by track

You can add or edit information directly in the main iTunes window by selecting the track and then clicking where you want to type. Any existing text will become highlighted and you're ready to go. When you're done, click somewhere else in the window or hit Enter.

Alternatively, to view, add or edit all kinds of information about a track, select it and click Get Info in the File or right-click menus.

Name	Artist	▲	Album
☑ Incubation	Joy Division		Substance
☑ Komakino	Joy Division		Substance
☑ Leaders Of Men	Joy Division		Substance
☑ Love Will Tear Us Apart	Joy Division		Substance
☑ No Love Lost	Joy Division		Substance
☑ Novelty	Joy Division		Substance
☑ She's Lost Control	**Get Info**		Substance
☑ These Days	Rating ▶		Substance
☑ Transmission	Show in Finder		Substance
☑ Warsaw	Create AAC Version		Unknown Ple
☑ Disorder	Create Ringtone...		Unknown Ple
☑ Day Of The Lords	Reset Play Count		Unknown Ple
☑ Candidate	Reset Skip Count		Unknown Ple
☑ Insight			Unknown Ple
☑ New Dawn Fades	Start Genius		Unknown Ple
☑ She's Lost Control	Play in iTunes DJ		Unknown Ple
☑ Shadowplay	Play Next in iTunes DJ		Unknown Ple
☑ Wilderness	Add to iTunes DJ		Unknown Ple
☑ Interzone			Unknown Ple
☑ I Remember Nothing	Uncheck Selection		Unknown Ple
☑ Hämmennys "Perplexcity"			Arctic Paradi
☑ Switch Out The Sun			Musiques Po

Selecting and editing multiple items

To edit information about multiple items simultaneously, you first need to select the tracks. This can be done in three ways:

▶ Hold down ⌘ (Mac) or Ctrl (PC) and click each song in turn.

▶ To select a bunch of adjacent tracks, click on the first and then Shift-click the last. Individual songs can then be removed from this selected group by clicking them while holding down ⌘ or Ctrl.

▶ Open the Browser (see p.128) and select an entire artist, album or genre. This is particularly handy when making sure your artists are tagged consistently. You might, for instance, select "N Cave" and "Nick Cave & The Bad Seeds", and change all those tracks to "Nick Cave".

Once that's done, click File > Get Info to display the Multiple Item Information box, where you can edit all the tracks' details at once. As soon as you make any changes, the box to the left of a specific text field becomes checked. Before you hit OK, make sure only the fields you want to change are checked.

Extra info

When editing track info, you can add all kinds of information in addition to the obvious stuff. Here are some tagging tips:

► **Comment** Use for any kind of additional information: personnel, producer, the instruments used, even full credits if you've got the time and inclination. This can be useful for both browsing and creating Smart Playlists.

► **Grouping** Like Comment, this is a useful wild-card category where you can create your own criteria for grouping and sorting songs. World music fans, for example, might enter a song's country of origin here; classical music fans might differentiate between century or instrument.

► **My Rating** This is where you get to play music reviewer and enter a 0–5 star rating of each song – great if you want to create a Smart Playlist of your favourite tracks.

> **TIP:** Tap the Select button on click-wheel iPods three times whilst playing a song and use the scroll wheel to add a star rating. On an iPod touch, double-tap the artwork of the currently playing song and then drag your finger across the five dots to add a rating. The stars will find their way back into iTunes next time you sync.

Track info shortcut keys

	Mac	PC
Open the track info window	⌘I	**Ctrl-I**
Show info for the next track in the Song List	⌘N	**Alt-N**
Show info for the previous track in the Song List	⌘P	**Alt-P**
Next pane in the track info window	⌘]	–
Previous pane in the track info window	⌘[	–

▶ **BPM** Lets you specify the tempo of the track, in beats per minute. This can be used to create DJ-style mixes. You could either arrange the tracks manually in a playlist, or sort a playlist by BPM and let iTunes do the mix with its "Crossfade" feature (see p.138). If you make your own music, BPM may also come in handy for picking songs of the right speed to sample.

▶ **Genres** Feel free to create your own genres, rather than sticking with those in the list. If you listen to jazz, say, you might want to use "bebop", "modal" and so on. Unlike when you use the Grouping field, your new genres will be easily accessible via the Browser (see p.128).

> **TIP:** If iTunes downloads incorrect or nonexistent song info and you have to do some manual entering or editing, select Submit CD Track Names from the iTunes Advanced menu once you're done. Then other people accessing the CDDB service will be able to benefit from your handiwork.

▶**Album Artist** This is useful for albums that have a main artist but feature tracks by, with or including other artists. Setting the main artist as the Album Artist for all the tracks on an album will ensure that all the songs stay together in the Browser, when sorting, and in your iTunes folder.

Alphabetizing

Select a single track and choose File > Get Info > Sorting. Here you'll find two columns of boxes. On the left are a few tags such as Artist and Album name; these simply reflect the details from the regular Song Info panel. To the right of each of these is another box where you can specify where the track should appear in lists sorted by the category in question. You might, for example, want the artist to *appear* as "Viktoria Mullova" but to be sorted by "Mullova, Viktoria", appearing under "M" rather than "V".

Summary	Info	Video	Sorting	Options	Lyrics	Artwork

Name	**Sort Name**
I. Allegro ma non troppo	Beethoven Violin Concerto I
Artist	**Sort Artist**
Viktoria Mullova	Mullova, Viktoria
Album Artist	**Sort Album Artist**

Tagging tools

If you want to do a repetitive tagging job – move all the Grouping entries to Comment for a particular artist, say, or put the entry for Title after the entry for Artist – there's probably a script or plug-in that will automate the process. For example, try "This Tag, That Tag" from Doug's Apple Scripts (dougscripts.com).

You can also search for duplicates in your Library – or specific playlists – by selecting Show Duplicate Songs in the Edit menu. Note, though, that this will only work if the artist and title info for the two versions are identical.

Select a tag to swap from:

- Song Name
- Artist
- Album
- Composer
- Genre
- Comments
- Grouping

Cancel   OK

TIP: To track down doubled up songs in iTunes, choose File > Show Duplicates. You can then choose which you want to keep and delete the clones.

Start/stop times

If you've ever been bugged by something at the beginning or end of a track – an extended fade, a concert recording applause, a snippet of indulgent band banter, or whatever – now is your chance to excise it. Whether you've ripped or downloaded the track, it can be topped and tailed in iTunes.

Take, for example, The Beatles' "Good Morning, Good Morning", which opens with the crow of a cockerel. If you listened to the song and kept an eye on the iTunes status area, you'd see that the cockerel's moment of glory lasts two seconds, and the band don't start playing until the display reads "Elapsed time: 0.03".

To erase the offending bird, simply select the track, choose File > Get Info > Options and enter a new Start Time of 0:03. Click OK and listen to the song again to see if the new setting is accurate. If not, go back and tweak the time, entering fractions of a second after a colon if necessary (eg 0:03:50).

Trimming the end works in just the same way. And whichever end you're changing, you're not harming the song file, only the way iTunes plays it, so none of this is permanent.

TIP: For more serious editing of tracks – from trimming them to combining them – you'll need to use an audio-editing program. See p.73.

Deleting files from iTunes

There are several ways to delete both music and video from the iTunes Library. But however you do it, first make sure that either Music, Movies or TV Shows (depending on what you are deleting) is selected in the Sources sidebar and then select the item or items you want to ditch in the main iTunes panel. Deleting items from a playlist (see p.58) does not delete the actual file from the iTunes Library – only the playlist's reference to the file.

   If you want to remove a whole album, artist or genre from your collection, open the Browser (see p.128) and select the relevant entry in the list. Then, either…

▶ **Hit Backspace or Delete** on your keyboard.

▶ **Select Clear** from the iTunes Edit menu.

▶ **Right-click (PC) or Ctrl-click (Mac)** the items and select Clear from the mouse menu.

▶ **Drag the selections straight to the Trash (Mac only)**

When asked, opt to send the files to the Trash, otherwise they'll remain in your iTunes folder, taking up space unnecessarily.

TIP: Deleting music as described above will send the files to your Recycle Bin or Trash, ready to be permanently deleted. If you want to remove something from iTunes but not delete it from your computer, the tidiest way is to select the song and choose File > Show in Finder or Windows Explorer to locate the file. Copy this file somewhere safe, then return to iTunes and remove the original. This way your iTunes folder will only contain files that are actually used by iTunes.

Managing your library

To find the actual file of any item in your iTunes library, select it, open the File menu and choose Show in Finder (on a Mac) or Show in Windows Explorer (on a PC).

By default, each file lives within a hierarchy of folders within your main iTunes folder, which in turn lives in your Music folder (Mac) or My Documents folder (PC). The hierarchy is defined by the artist, album and album artist details of the tracks. For example, The Beatles' "Dig A Pony" would usually be found here:

iTunes ▶ iTunes Music ▶ The Beatles ▶ Let It Be ▶ Dig A Pony

Consolidating

In some circumstances, you may find that certain tracks are located outside your iTunes folder. If you'd rather have all the tracks neatly arranged in one place, use the Library > Consolidate Library… option in the File menu. This will copy all the files into your iTunes folder.

Moving your "iTunes Music" folder

If, say, your computer is running out of disk space, you may want to move all your music and video files (which all live together in the "iTunes Music" folder) onto an external hard drive connected to your computer by either USB or FireWire. To do this, follow the following procedure:

▶ **Open iTunes Preferences** and under the Advanced tab check the "Keep iTunes Music folder organized" box. Then click OK.

▶ **Open Preferences > Advanced again** and click the Change button. Then browse for the location where you want the iTunes Music folder to live, click the New Folder button, and name it something like "iTunes Music II". Click OK twice to close the panels.

▶**Then consolidate** Choose Library > Consolidate Library from the File menu to move all your files … this might take a while.

▶ **Delete the old folder** When iTunes has finished copying everything over, locate the old "iTunes Music" folder (not to be confused with the "iTunes" folder; see below) and delete it.

Note that this process will leave the "iTunes" folder, album art-work, etc, where it was and also not effect your playlists.

Moving the whole "iTunes" folder

It's also relatively easy to move your whole "iTunes" folder (com-plete with all playlist information, album artwork, the iTunes library database, apps, etc) to another location – another compu-ter, an external hard drive, or even somewhere else on the same machine. Follow this procedure:

▶ **Quit iTunes** on the machine you are moving the folder from.

▶ **Copy the iTunes folder** to the desired new location. This may take a while. When moving the folder to another machine, you can first copy it to an external drive or DVD and then to the second machine.

▶ **Launch iTunes** whilst holding down Alt (mac) or Shift (PC). The Choose iTunes Library window appears; select "Choose Library…" and navigate to the new location of the folder; select it and hit Open.

If you intend to keep your library on an external drive, you'll need to power up and connect the drive before starting iTunes. If you don't, iTunes will display the "Choose iTunes Library" box pictured opposite.

> **TIP:** If you intend to keep either your "iTunes" or "iTunes Music" folders on an external hard drive, it will need to be connected and powered up each time you launch iTunes.

Converting music formats

iTunes allows you to create new versions of tracks in different file formats or at different bitrates. You might want to convert a bulky WAV file into a space-efficient AAC, for example, or create a low-quality copy of a track to send by email.

Note that converting files from one compressed format to another – from MP3 to AAC, say – might effect the sound quality. Each compression format works by removing different details from the soundwave, so even if MP3 and AAC both sound great, a track that has undergone both compressions may not. So don't delete the original unless you've checked the converted file for fidelity.

To convert a track, first specify your desired format and bitrate under iTunes Preferences > General > Import Settings. Then select the track or tracks and choose Advanced > Convert Selection To…

> **TIP:** If iTunes won't let you convert a file, it may have embedded DRM protection. You may be able to get around this by burning the file to CD and then re-ripping it in a different format. However, this may break the terms of your user licence, depending on where you got the track. The same is true of the various converting programs (see p.93) that you can easily find online. For more info, see: mp3-converter.com.

16

Album artwork

Putting the cover into Cover Flow

Back in the early days of the digital music revolution, one thing conspicuous by its absence was album artwork. Thankfully, the situation has been improved by various developments: colour-screen iPods that can display album sleeves; Cover Flow view, which lets you flick through your virtual artwork collection; and the iTunes Store which these days provides artwork not only for music it sells, but also for tracks you've ripped from CD.

> **TIP:** If you don't want album artwork on your iPod, uncheck the relevant option under the Music tab of the iPod Options panel in iTunes.

Clicking the title bar of the panel toggles between showing artwork for the Selected Song and Now Playing song.

Clicking the fourth button below the Sources sidebar reveals and hides the artwork panel.

Automatically adding artwork

Under the Store tab of the iTunes Preferences panel is a check box to "Automatically download missing album artwork", which *should* enable iTunes to search the iTunes Store database for the album artwork that you need, at the time at which you import tracks from either a CD or other source.

You can also select one or more tracks – or even your entire collection – and choose Get Album Artwork from the Advanced menu. Be warned, though, that it can take a while to process a large number of tracks, and iTunes has been known to throw up some strange results, with the wrong artwork coming through or new artwork overwriting existing, manually added covers.

> **TIP:** Though you won't have to pay to use cover art, you will need an iTunes Store account (see p.99) to search for artwork automatically through iTunes.

Manually adding artwork

It's also possible to manually add artwork, by looting it from the Internet or even scanning it. There are various ways to do this:

▶ Select one or more tracks and drag or paste an image into the iTunes Artwork panel (pictured opposite).

▶ Select a track and choose File > Get Info > Artwork > Add…

▶ Select multiple tracks, choose File > Get Info and double-click the white Artwork box.

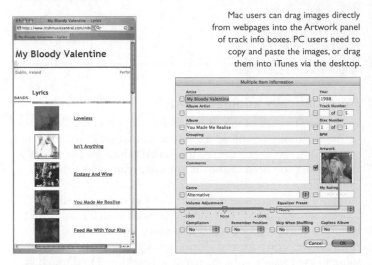

Mac users can drag images directly from webpages into the Artwork panel of track info boxes. PC users need to copy and paste the images, or drag them into iTunes via the desktop.

Finding artwork online

Most sleeves can be found online via a Google Image Search. You can either right-click the image and copy it or drag it onto your desktop as a file. However, bear the following in mind:

▶ **Google thumbs** When browsing the results of a Google image search, don't use the thumbnail of the cover that Google presents you with, instead click through to the full-sized version.

▶ **Size matters** Try to find versions of the album art that are at least 300x300 pixels (Google displays dimensions below its thumbnail

Where are the pictures?

Confusingly, there are two ways in which artwork can be associated with your music in iTunes. The image can be either:

▶ **Added to the Album Artwork folder** Found in the main iTunes folder, the Album Artwork folder contains the artwork associated with albums rather than individual tracks. This is where iTunes puts images it has gathered automatically.

▶ **Embedded in the song file** It's also possible to embed an image within a music (or video) file, and this is what happens when you add artwork manually to one or more selections. The advantage of this technique is that even if the iTunes Album Artwork folder is damaged or deleted, or if you drag a file out of iTunes, the artwork remains intact.

Because there are two ways of storing images, you may often find that, even though a song has an album in Cover Flow, no image appears in the Artwork panel or the track info box (pictured).

Mac users can get around this by using an AppleScript (*dougscripts .com/itunes*) to automatically embed the covers from the iTunes Album Artwork folder into all the individual tracks of those albums.

What am I missing?

There are a couple of ways to get a handle on what album artwork you might be missing. If you run the automatic iTunes artwork-gathering command from the Advanced menu, you will be offered, as it finishes, a list of all the albums for which artwork could not be found. Hit the Save button to create a text document of the information which you can refer to when filling in the gaps manually.

The second method, available to Mac-users only, is to run an AppleScript that creates a new playlist containing tracks without embedded artwork. To download the script, visit *dougscripts.com/itunes* and look for the Managing Artwork link.

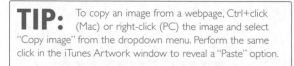

TIP: To copy an image from a webpage, Ctrl+click (Mac) or right-click (PC) the image and select "Copy image" from the dropdown menu. Perform the same click in the iTunes Artwork window to reveal a "Paste" option.

previews), as anything smaller will look poor when viewing Cover Flow (see p.130) in full-screen mode.

▶ **Other searches** If you can't find what you want via Google Images, try a regular Google search for the artist's name plus the word "discography". CD stores' and record labels' sites can also be useful.

▶ **eBay** If you get really stuck, eBay can be handy for locating either photographs or scans of obscure old singles and albums.

There are also third-party applications available that'll do all the hard work for you: to find out more, turn to p.240.

TIP: If there's a sleeve you can't find anywhere – or you have a radio session or some other track that has never been released with cover art – then be creative and find or design something suitable.

17

Burning CDs & DVDs

Creating a hard copy

I f you have an iPod or computer hooked up to a hi-fi or a decent set of speakers, then there's little need to put your carefully compiled playlists onto CD for use at home. However, if you want to give a compilation to a friend, you'll need to burn it onto CD (or, possibly, give them the original music files; see p.91). Burning DVDs can also be a useful way to back up your music.

Stage 1: pick your disc

CD options

If you have a CD burner on your computer, it will usually allow you to burn two types of CD disc: CDR (which you can burn only once) and CDRW (which can be written onto many times). You can burn onto these discs in various different ways, creating:

▶ **Regular audio CDs** for playing back on standard hi-fis. These can hold around 74–80 minutes of music, depending on the disc. Use CDR, not CDRW, for burning normal music discs, as they're less likely to refuse to play back on home stereos.

▶ **MP3 CDs** can store around 10–12 hours of music, but they can only include tracks in MP3 format (see p.65) and can only be played back on computers or special MP3 CD players. Again, use CDR, not CDRW, discs.

> **TIP:** If most of your tracks are in the default iTunes AAC format and you want to burn them to an MP3 CD, you'll first have to convert them to MP3 (see p.155).

▶ **Data CDs** hold music as computer files, so they can only be read by computers and a few clever hi-fis. They let you store about 650–750MB of music (around 10–12 hours, depending on the sound quality) in any file format, so are useful for moving large volumes of music between computers. Both CDR and CDRW discs are suitable.

DVD options

If your computer has a DVD burner that's compatible with iTunes, you can also create Data DVDs. These work just like data CDs, except that they can hold much more data (in most cases around 4.5GB) and can only be read by computers with DVD drives.

Burning video DVDs

Though iTunes can burn a data DVD, it can't create a video DVD for playback on regular household DVD players. However, this can be done with some other software that you probably already have: iDVD, which most Mac users will find in their Applications folder; and DVD Maker, which PC users will find in the Windows programs list.

iDVD is neatly integrated with iTunes, offering direct access to your video collection via the Media tab. DVD Maker lacks this integration, so PC users will need to locate their iTunes video files in Window Explorer, as described on p.153:

iDVD apple.com/iDVD
Windows DVD Maker windowsdvdmaker.com

Useful for backing up, these can be created on either DVDR or DVDRW discs.

Stage 2: Assemble a playlist

To burn a disc in iTunes – even a data disc – you first need to arrange the relevant tracks into a playlist. As you drag songs into the list, the statistics at the bottom of the window will tell you the total running time and file size of the selections added so far. You'll need to limit yourself to 74–80 minutes for a standard audio CD, or 650–700 megabytes for a data or MP3 CD. The discs or their packaging should state the capacity.

If you can't resist adding more tracks than will fit on a disc, don't fret: iTunes will just burn what it can and then prompt you to insert a second disc to accommodate what's left over.

TIP: You can also burn a CD from a Smart Playlist. However, its contents may be different from one day to the next, so if you like the selection enough to put it on disc, burn it there and then or copy the tracks into a regular playlist.

Stage 3: Burn...

When you're ready to roll, select the playlist in question and click Burn Disc at the bottom-right corner of the iTunes window. (Alternatively, select Burn Playlist to Disc from the File or right-click menus.) The Burn Settings box then appears:

Burning Settings

Here, choose the type of disc that you want to burn. You can also specify a preferred burning speed: leave it set to Maximum Possible, unless your machine is struggling to burn a disc success-fully. If you're creating a standard audio CD, you can also choose from these extra options:

▶ **Sound Check** will alter the volume levels to equalize the loudness of the various tracks on the disc (see box opposite).

▶ **Gap Between Songs** doesn't require much explanation, though it's worth noting that these extra seconds aren't included in iTunes' estimation of the length of your playlist.

Burn Settings

CD Burner: MATSHITA DVD-R UJ-875

Preferred Speed: Maximum Possible

Disc Format: ● Audio CD
  Gap Between Songs: none
  ☐ Use Sound Check
  ☑ Include CD Text
  ○ MP3 CD
  ○ Data CD or DVD
  Data discs include all files in the playlist. These discs may not play in some players.

Cancel   Burn

Sound Check and other options

The Sound Check function has a stab at equalizing the volume levels between tracks so that when you play back your new CD one song won't be ear-splittingly loud compared to another. This function works fine for most differences in sound level, but if you find that the songs you've combined are still irritatingly dispa- rate on playback, try adjusting the volumes of individual tracks using the iTunes "Volume Adjustment" function (see p.175).

If that doesn't do the trick then perhaps you need to return to the source (was one song ripped from a CD and another imported from an analogue medium?) and try to figure out why a particular song has such a low noise level. Alternatively, use some audio-editing software (see p.73) to boost the volume of the quiet files.

▶ **Include CD Text** This basically embeds the tracklisting information onto the CD so that it shows up when the disc is inserted into a CD that can handle CD Text. Car stereos often make use of this feature to display the currently playing selection on a scrolling panel. Even if you don't think this is relevant to you, keep it checked, as it won't slow down the burn and will add a little more compatibility to the disc you are creating.

When you are happy with the settings, hit Burn, and the iTunes status window will prompt you to insert a blank disc, which it will quickly check over before it starts to burn the disc. The burning process will take a few minutes, depending upon the speed of your hardware and the size of the playlist. When iTunes has finished, the CD will appear in the iTunes Sources sidebar ready to be played or ejected.

TIP: If you want iTunes to eject CDs after burning them, check Import CD And Eject in iTunes Preferences > General > On CD Insert. This will also cause CDs to be automatically ripped when inserted.

Burning problems

If you're having problems burning a CD or DVD using iTunes, check the following:

▶ **Is your drive supported?** Some CD and DVD drives that didn't come built in to an Apple computer are not compatible with iTunes. If your drive is correctly listed within the Burn Settings box (pictured on p.164), it should, theoretically, be fine.

▶ **Does your computer go to sleep while you burn?** To stop this from happening in OS X, open System Preferences and within the Energy Saver pane increase the time before your computer sleeps. On a PC this is done in the Control Panel under Power Management.

▶ **Are you burning the right type of files?** If burning an MP3 CD, you can only include songs in MP3 format. Turning on the Kind column (see p.127) in the main iTunes pane lets you see which tracks are in which format.

▶ **Have the songs been authorized?** If iTunes refuses to burn a song on the grounds that it hasn't been authorized to play on your computer, you'll need to double-click the song in question and enter the iTunes ID and password for the account (see p.99) through which the songs were purchased.

Finally, if you successfully created a CD but it won't work on one or more hi-fis, double-check that you are burning a regular audio CD onto a CDR disc. If so, it could just be that your hi-fi is incompatible with computer-created CDs. Try burning the CD using a different brand of CDR, and if that doesn't work either, you know it's the hi-fi that has the problem.

Making covers

Half the joy of assembling a compilation has always been the painstaking process of making the cover. Doing this on a computer may not have the same romance about it, but at least you don't have to manually write out all the artist and track names – and with a half-decent printer you can create some pretty professional-looking results.

With iTunes

To create a cover using the iTunes built-in tools, select the playlist that you've just burned – or choose a genre, artist or album in the Browser – and select Print from the File menu or with the keyboard shortcuts ⌘P (Mac) or Ctrl-P (PC). A box will pop up offering various options for printing the track name and album art, where relevant, as either a regular document or an insert for a CD jewel case. If and when you are happy with how the cover or sheet looks (you can get a full-sized view by clicking Print and then Preview), choose Page Setup to assign printer-specific options and then hit Print.

Other programs

This is all very handy, but rather artistically limiting. Another option is to export your playlist's track names as a text document, and then paste them into another program that will allow you more creativity over the cover. To do this, select a playlist and then choose Export Playlist… from the File menu or right-click menu. A box appears where you can choose to save the file as a text document or an XML document.

> **TIP:** Whatever software you intend to use to make your covers – be it Microsoft Word or Photoshop – you should be able to find various CD templates ready to download and fill in online. Try searching Google for "CD", "templates" and the name of your program.

Extra tools

There are a number of third-party tools and scripts that can help you to create CD covers. For example, the free iTunes Publisher lets you export playlists in various formats, including tabbed text, Winamp and HTML. Or try the "Playlist to papercdcase.com" script from Doug's AppleScripts.

iTunes Publisher trancesoftware.com
Doug's AppleScripts dougscripts.com

Tweaking
the sound

EQ and beyond

As we've seen, one way to enhance the sound on your
computer and iPod is to be discerning with your import
preferences (see p.61). Another is to improve your speakers,
either by investing in better earphones for your Pod (see
p.231) or by hooking up to a decent hi-fi (see p.177). Aside
from all this, you can also tweak the sound using various iTunes
tools, including a pretty comprehensive graphic equalizer. You
can either apply EQ as you listen, or assign customized presets
to specific tracks, which are then transported to your iPod
when you next sync.

Equalizing

All sound is made up of vibrations. Deep bass sounds are produced at low frequencies – as little as 32 hertz (vibrations per second) – while high-pitched sounds result from frequencies as high as 16 kilohertz (16,000 cycles per second).

Music produced by acoustic instruments consists of a complex and dynamic combination of frequencies. To get the optimum sound, you can tweak the relative volume of different frequencies according to your taste, your speakers, the recording quality and even the shape of the room you're in.

Most stereos let you boost or suppress high and low frequencies under the broad titles of "treble" and "bass". For more control, however, you need a graphic equalizer, which breaks the sound into many frequency bands to let you tweak the overall "EQ" of the sound. Luckily, there's one built right in to iTunes…

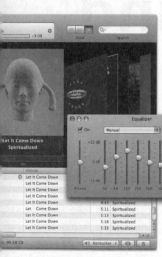

iTunes Equalizer

To switch on the iTunes Equalizer, open it from the View (PC) or Window (Mac) menu and check the "On" box. Experiment with the various frequency sliders and the Preamp, which affects the overall

TIP: On a Mac, you can also open the Equalizer by using the keyboard shortcut ⌘⌥2.

volume. Note that once the Equalizer is switched on, the window *doesn't* need to be open for the settings to take effect.

> **TIP:** If boosting individual frequency bands with the Equalizer causes distortion, lower the Preamp setting to between -6db and -12db, and then compensate by increasing your computer's master volume level.

Presets

From the Equalizer's dropdown menu you can choose between a number of preset frequency settings, designed to suit different types of music. "Dance", for example, has boosted bass, while "Spoken Word" features stronger mid-range frequencies, just like the human voice. Play some music you are familiar with and try out a few presets. Check and uncheck the "On" box to compare the new setting to the unequalized original.

Make your own presets

At any time you can drag the sliders up and down yourself to try to get a sound perfectly matched to the music you're listening to (as you do so, the Preset dropdown will display Manual).

TIP: When constructing your own EQ presets, start with the "Flat" preset and build on that: you'll get a much better feel for the effect each of your additional drags is having on the original sound.

If you create an EQ you like, you can save it by selecting "Make Preset…" from the dropdown and choosing a name.

Once you've made a preset, you can recall it at any time by clicking its entry in the dropdown menu. You can also edit, rename or delete any preset by choosing Edit List… from the dropdown menu.

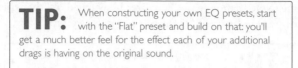

Applying EQ presets to songs

So far we've looked at using the Equalizer as a real-time tool, simply changing the settings and presets as you listen. However, iTunes also allows you to assign EQ presets to specific songs so that both iTunes and your iPod know exactly how you want to hear them. First, select a song or songs and choose Get Info from the File menu. Next, turn to the Equalizer Preset dropdown menu (found within Options when you're dealing with a single song), and choose from the list.

And on to the Pod…

All your individual song EQ settings are carried over to the iPod when you sync. However, the iPod also allows you to apply presets manually at any time – look under Settings > EQ (click-wheel models) or Settings > Music > EQ (iPod touch).

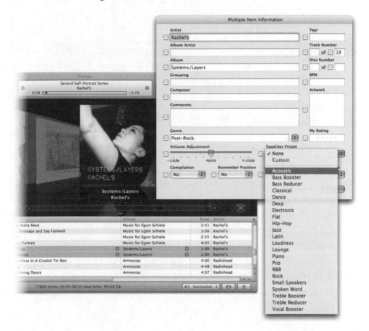

Also look out for the iPod's Sound Check function, also under Settings (click-wheel models) and Settings > Music (iPod touch), which can be toggled on and off. However, the single best way to improve the sound that comes out of your iPod is to buy a decent pair of sound-isolating earphones (see p.231).

Other sound settings

As well as EQ, iTunes offers a couple of other sound-tweaking settings within the Playback pane of iTunes Preferences.

Sound Enhancer

In theory, when you set the Sound Enhancer to high you should notice a general improvement of the "presence" in the music you play. It's tricky to quantify, but the sound should be brighter and the stereo separation more vivid. You may not like the effect – or not be able to tell the difference – but it's certainly worth experimenting with, so check the box, slide the slider and see what you think.

Sound Enhancer is usually most beneficial for compressed audio formats like MP3 and AAC, but you may also notice a difference with CD playback. The only real downside is that it can keep your computer's processor pretty busy, which could result in glitches and skips on slower machines.

Sound Check

When Sound Check is on, iTunes attempts to play back all songs at approximately the same volume level, so you shouldn't have to keep turning the sound up and down as you jump around your collection. As more songs are added to your Library, iTunes recalculates its setting and stores the information in its database. It's

Volume Adjustment

To boost or lower the volume of a particular track, select it, choose Get Info from the File menu and, in the box that pops up, click Options to reveal the Volume Adjustment slider. iTunes saves your setting and will use it whenever the song is played – including on an iPod. You can apply Volume Adjustment to multiple tracks simultaneously, or even to whole albums, artists or genres by selecting them in the Browser (see p.128) and clicking File > Get Info.

not perfect, and you may still notice discrepancies in loudness between different songs, especially where songs have been import- ed from a non-CD source. If particular tracks are still too quiet or too loud, use the Volume Adjustment setting to bring them into line (see box above).

Third-party plug-ins

The iTunes sound features are pretty good, but if you want even more you'll find plenty of programs and plug-ins on the Net. Among the best is iWOW Premium, which is available for both Mac and PC, though it will set you back $50.

iWOW Premium srslabs.com

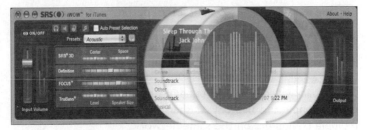

19

iPodding your home

Connecting to hi-fis, speakers and televisions

The iPod does an excellent job of putting music and video in your pocket. But when you want to listen or watch at home, a pair of earphones and a matchbox-sized screen are not ideal. Instead, consider connecting your iPod or computer to a hi-fi or a stand-alone speaker system for music, or to a TV for playing back video. This chapter explains the various ways this can be done – and also covers sharing music and video between multiple computers on the same network.

Connecting to a hi-fi

Though there are some excellent stand-alone speakers on the market (see p.232), it's also possible to connect an iPod or computer to regular hi-fis. Connecting an iPod is neat and convenient, whereas connecting a computer gives you better controls.

All you need is a hi-fi with a "line-in" – look on the back for an unused pair of red and white RCA sockets. They may be labelled Aux or Line-in, though any input other than Phono (which will have a built-in preamp) should be fine. If your stereo doesn't have a line-in, try an using its radio and an FM transmitter (see p.226).

Computer to hi-fi by cable

Nearly all computers have line-out or headphone minijack sockets. So if your computer and stereo are in the same room, you can pick up an inexpensive RCA-to-minijack cable and run it straight from the computer to the hi-fi. If your computer and hi-fi are further apart or in different rooms, you could buy a long cable and get the drill out, but you might prefer to investigate a wireless setup.

The DAC alternative

If iTunes has become the main music source within your household you might decide to upgrade your hi-fi set-up to reflect this fact. There are now several excellent DAC (digital to audio converter) amp and speaker systems on the market that connect directly to your PC or Mac via USB and take the burden of audio processing away from your computer. This should result in both superior fidelity and an increase in your computer's overall performance. Of the models we've tested, the NuForce Icon2 combo is by far the best.

NuForce nuforce-icon.com

Computer to hi-fi wirelessly

If your hi-fi has a line-in, but you don't
want to be limited by cables – perhaps you
have a laptop or your computer is in a different room from your stereo – investigate
Apple's AirPort Express wireless base station (pictured).

Attach one of these to a power point and
connect it to your hi-fi with a standard
RCA-to-minijack cable. Then, any computer on the same Wi-Fi network can beam
music straight to the hi-fi, even from the
other side of the house.

> **TIP:** If no signal seems to be getting from your PC or
> Mac to your hi-fi, check the volume is turned up
> in iTunes, on the computer, and on the hi-fi.

If your computer doesn't have Wi-Fi, you can add it inexpensively with the appropriate internal, external or PCMCIA device.
Ask in any computer store or see *The Rough Guide to the Internet*
for more information.

To send music to an AirPort Express unit, first check "Look for
remote speakers…" in the Devices section of iTunes Preferences.
All AirPort Express units in range should then appear in a dropdown menu on the bottom of the iTunes window. You can either
choose one or click Multiple Speakers… to play through more
than one simultaneously.

> **TIP:** For a truly minimal wireless music system,
> unencumbered by such old-fashioned
> equipment as a hi-fi, combine an AirPort Express with a pair
> of powered speakers (see p.233).

An AirPort Express also acts as a wireless Internet router and lets you connect to printers wirelessly. And, with third-party applications Airfoil and Airfoil Speakers, you can use your AirPort Express to stream audio from other applications as well as iTunes.

AirPort Express apple.com/airportexpress
Airfoil rogueamoeba.com/airfoil $25 (Mac & PC)

iPod touch users might also be interested to know that the company that make Airfoil also make an iPod app called Airfoil Speakers Touch that can be used to stream audio from any program on your Mac or PC to an iPod touch, to all intents and purposes giving it the same functionality as an AirPort Express unit. Dowmload it for free from the App Store (see p.119).

> **TIP:** Though you can't stream music directly from the iPod touch (which has built-in Wi-Fi) to an AirPort Express, you can use Apple's Remote app to control the stream of music flowing from your computer to connected wireless speakers. For more, see p.241.

Other Wi-Fi music receivers

There are many non-Apple devices that do a similar job to the AirPort Express. Some boast additional features, such as a display, Ethernet ports, Internet radio streaming and remote controls. However, note that they won't play songs purchased from the iTunes Store unless you go to the hassle of burning and re-ripping them (see the tip on p.155). Some popular brands include:

Squeezebox slimdevices.com
SoundBridge rokulabs.com
HomePod macsense.com

iPod to hi-fi by cable

A Pod doesn't give you quite the ease of use and flexibility of iTunes, but it's small, silent and doesn't require you to run a cable across your room. Simply run an RCA-to-minijack cable between your hi-fi's line-in and your Pod's headphone socket or, better still, the Line Out socket on the back of an iPod Dock, as pictured below. The Dock solution can be made all the more convenient when combined with a wireless remote control (see p.234).

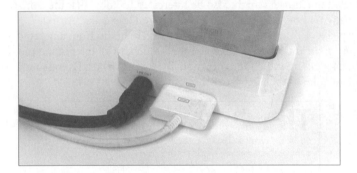

iPod to hi-fi via FM radio

An FM transmitter plugs into the headphone socket on your iPod (many will also plug into a computer) and beams the sound around the room as an FM radio signal. Then your stereo can tune in just as it would to any other radio station.

Though you won't get particularly high-fidelity sound and your stereo or iPod will need to be relatively close to your radio, this can still be a very convenient solution, allowing you to walk around the house zapping music from your Pod to any nearby radio. It's also the only easy way to connect to a hi-fi that lacks a line-in socket. For recommended models, see p.226.

Connecting to TVs

Depending on its screen and its location in the home, your computer may already be perfectly situated for watching your downloading or ripped movies and TV shows. In many cases, however, it's preferable to play them on a regular TV set.

You could always use some extra software to burn the files onto a video DVD (see p.163), but there are various other solutions…

iPod to TV

All iPods capable of playing movie files on their screens (see pp.26–29) can also play video through a connected TV, though don't expect amazing quality. To connect an iPod to a TV, you could purchase the Apple-produced iPod AV cable ($19/£15), but it's less expensive to buy a generic cable with standard yellow/red/white RCA connectors at one end and a three-banded minijack at the other. These look very similar to Apple's AV cable, but will only work with an iPod if you shuffle the colours around when you connect to the TV:

AV cable white ► **TV jack red**
AV cable red ► **TV jack yellow**
AV cable yellow ► **TV jack white**

If you have an older Apple Universal Dock, you might also be able to connect using an S-video cable, though newer Apple Universal Docks (see p.228) don't feature an S-video port.

Once your iPod is hooked up, look within the Settings menu for the Video Settings, and turn on TV Out.

> **TIP:** You can also view photos stored on an iPod on a TV screen using the appropriate cable. To find out how, see p.80.

Computer to TV

It's always been possible to buy adapters and cables to connect computers to televisions. This can still be done, though a neater solution emerged in 2007 with the launch of the Apple TV – or simply **tv**.

The device, compatible with Macs and PCs, connects to your TV via a cable and to your computer via your wireless network. It can import files from iTunes to its own internal hard drive for playback on the TV, or stream them directly from your computer in real time. It can also be granted access to the Internet, allowing you to rent movies from the iTunes Store (see p.102), watch free movie trailers, and browse YouTube (though not the rest of the

What you need

Apple TV will only work with enhanced- or high-definition televisions capable of displaying 1080i 60/50Hz, 720p 60/50Hz, 576p 50Hz (PAL format) or 480p 60Hz. This includes most flat-screen televisions purchased since 2006 – including all those with an HD-ready logo – but not many older models.

You'll also need the right cables (not supplied) and the right sockets to connect them to. The basic option is a component video cable (three phono-like connectors coloured red, green and blue) plus a phono or optical cable for the audio. If you have the right port, you could use an HDMI cable instead. These offer excellent video and audio quality all-in-one, but they're very expensive.

For more details about Apple TV connection requirements, go to: *apple.com/appletv/connect.html*.

Web) on your TV. Playback is controlled with an infrared remote
control and an on-screen menu system similar to that of Front
Row (see p.184).

Once set up, the Apple TV appears in iTunes with a series of tabs allowing you to choose which videos you want to copy across to the device. You can also browse your entire iTunes Library direct from Apple TV and stream the files in real time. This is fine for music, but depending on the speed of your network, not ideal for video.

TIP: If using an Apple TV for television shows stored
in iTunes, the best option is "Sync all unwatched
episodes". This way, they'll be deleted from the Apple TV as
soon as they've been viewed. To reinstate an episode, select it
in iTunes and choose File > "Mark as New".

Preparing your video files

All video downloaded from the iTunes Store will work with an
Apple TV – and they can look surprisingly good, despite their
relatively low resolutions. Video from other sources will need to
be prepared using the "Convert Selection for Apple TV" option in
the iTunes Advanced menu. For ripping DVDs, HandBrake (see
p.85) features an Apple TV preset.

Note that video files converted for Apple TV *won't* play back on
iPods. Files prepared for iPods *will* play back on an Apple TV, but
they don't look quite so good.

Front Row

If you have a Mac that came with a remote control, you'll also have Front Row – OS X's full-screen media-player mode. You can use Front Row to access music and video from your iTunes library, play inserted DVDs, browse your iPhoto collection and even access online movie trailers.

If you have an older Mac, without an Apple Remote but with OS X 10.4.8 or later, you can unlock Front Row and control it using the following keyboard shortcuts. Combined with a wireless keyboard this can be almost as useful. To find out how, see andrewescobar.com/frontrow.

⌘-Esc Show and hide Front Row
↑ and ↓ Scroll through menus
⌥↑ and ⌥↓ Adjust volume level
Enter or Space Select/play/pause/resume
Esc Back to previous menu or screen

Combining multiple computers with Front Row and an AirPort Express can allow you to control your music in many different ways. For example, you might have a desktop PC in the study which houses your iTunes Library. If you have sharing enabled (see opposite), you could access this collection via Front Row on a Mac laptop in the kitchen and have the music streamed to a pair of speakers in any room you like via an AirPort Express.

Sharing

If you have two or more computers on a home network (for example, if you share your Internet connection via a wireless router), then each machine can access the iTunes collection of the others. First, however, you need to set the sharing options for each computer by opening iTunes Preferences from the iTunes or Edit menus and looking under the Sharing tab.

Here, you can instruct your computer to share its library (or just selected playlists) and/or look for other libraries on the network.

Next, decide if you want to set a password for others accessing your songs: this isn't compulsory, but it could be useful if, say, you're embarrassed about your easy listening playlist. When you're done, click OK and start sharing.

Connecting and disconnecting

Once you've set up two computers to share, their icons should appear in each other's Sources sidebar, as shown below. Click the icon to view the contents, or tap the small triangle to the left of the shared library's icon to reveal any playlists.

LIBRARY	Genre	Artist		
♫ Music	All (97 Genres)	All (1970 Artists)		
▣ Movies	Alt Rock/Indie	Podcasts		
▣ TV Shows	Alt. Rock	A.A. Gray & Seven-Foot Dilly		
▣ Podcasts	Alternative			
▣ Radio	**Name**	**Time**	**Artist** ▲	**Bit R**
STORE	☑ The Old Ark's A Moving	2:58	A.A. Gray & Seven-...	320 kb
▣ iTunes Store	☑ Take1 (Clean)	4:04	–A+M	192 kb
SHARED	☑ Take1 (Megaphone)	4:04	–A+M	192 kb
▶ ▣ Peter Buckley's... ⏏	☑ Take2	6:28	–A+M	192 kb
▼ PLAYLISTS	☑ Love is an arrow	2:14	Aberfeldy	128 kb
▣ Party Shuffle	☑ Summer's Gone	3:33	Aberfeldy	192 kb
▣ 90's Music	☑ Vegetarian restaur	3:17	Aberfeldy	192 kb
▣ Music Videos	☑ A Friend Like You	2:59	Aberfeldy	160 kb
▣ My Top Rated	☑ Tie One On	3:50	Aberfeldy	192 kb
	☑ What You Do	4:48	Aberfeldy	160 kb
	☑ Young Forever	1:45	Aberfeldy	160 kb
	☑ Heliopolis By Night	3:18	Aberfeldy	160 kb

When you've finished with someone else's library, you can "eject" it to remove it from your iTunes window. To do this, hit the eject icon next to the shared library's icon or in the bottom-right of the iTunes window.

Sharing limitations

iTunes sharing has certain in-built limitations: you can't copy or burn music from other computers, nor add it to your iPod. And, of course, computers have to be switched on to be accessible. If you'd rather permanently copy music files from machine to machine, see p.90 for advice.

Extras

20

iPod as hard drive

Moving and backing up files

Though they may have revolutionized the way we listen to music, iPods are, at the end of the day, little more than glorified data-storage devices in pretty little boxes. The iPod classic and most older iPods contain hard drives just like those found in computers, albeit a touch smaller. Other models – shuffles, nanos and the touch – use standard Flash memory. Little wonder, then, that iPods can be used to store all types of computer files. Indeed, if you have some free space on your Pod, you can use it for anything from backing up key files to transferring documents between home and the office. And it will still play music and video as usual.

Enabling hard drive use

To use your iPod as a hard drive, first you have to enable this feature. Simply connect it to your computer and, within the Summary or Settings pane in iTunes, check the Enable Disk Use box. If you're using an iPod shuffle you'll also need to use the slider to specify how much space you'd like to allocate to disk mode, and how much to reserve for music.

Don't worry about the "manual unmounting" warning that may pop up – it's only telling you that you'll now have to eject the Pod (see p.48) each time you want to disconnect it.

Moving files between Macs and PCs

When you first plug an iPod into your computer, it prepares it for use by formatting the hard drive. iPods formatted on a PC can be recognized by both PCs and Macs, which is great if you're using your iPod as a hard drive, as it means you can move files between nearly all computers. However, iPods formatted on Macs can *not* be recognized by PCs.

So, if you're a Mac user who intends to use your iPod on both platforms (either to transfer files or update music manually), consider reformatting it on a PC by attaching it to the PC and clicking Restore in the Summary area of iTunes. This will delete all content from the iPod, but everything can be synced back over next time you connect to your Mac.

Using your drive

Once disk use is enabled, your iPod will appear as a standard drive whenever you connect it to your computer. On a Mac you'll find it on the Desktop and Sidebar (pictured). On a PC, it will appear in My Computer with an identification letter such as "F:" or "G:".

You can use the drive as you would any other – view its contents (though your music will be invisible), create folders, drag files on, drag files off. And so on.

You'll probably find several folders in the iPod's drive when you open it: these relate to iPod organizer and photo functions and should be left alone.

Deleting files

As with any other external hard drive, it is worth noting that when you delete files, or folders of files, from your iPod they are moved

One for Mac geeks – the iPod startup disk

Do you own a Mac laptop? Are you technically minded? Then you could try installing the recovery software that came with your Mac onto your iPod. This would give you a useful means of restarting and repairing your computer if it ever died when you were out and about and you didn't have the CDs to hand. You can even go the whole way and install a fully working OS to your Pod, though it may never play music again. Both these activities are beyond the scope of this book, but if you fancy giving them a go, look online for tips and advice. For a list of relevant websites, see p.261.

to the Recycle Bin (PC) or Trash (Mac). Although they no longer appear on the iPod, the space that they were occupying cannot be used for anything else until you empty your Recycle Bin or Trash.

Ejecting

When you are done with the drive, eject ("dismount") it in the normal way (see p.48).

21

iPod as organizer

Contacts, calendars, alerts and alarms

As music and video players, iPods are superb. As portable hard drives, they're excellent. As personal organizers, however, most iPods are rather more basic. One exception is the iPod touch, which doubles as a useful address book and diary. Other iPods can *display* contact and calendar information, but not create entries or edit existing details. This can still be useful, though – for example, to provide alerts when appointments are imminent. In addition, all iPods can wake you up in the morning with a playlist of your choice.

Contacts & calendars

Getting contacts and calendars onto your click-wheel or iPod touch from your computer is in most cases made easy by iTunes. Simply connect your iPod and look under either the Contacts tab for click-wheel Pods or Info tab if you have an iPod touch. Here's a brief look at how you might sync things from various common programs and online services:

▶**Address Book & iCal (Mac)** iTunes can sync Address Book and iCal automatically. Simply connect your iPod and set the options within iTunes.

▶ **Outlook & Outlook Express (PC)** iTunes can automatically transfer Outlook contacts and calendars, and Outlook Express contacts, to an iPod. Connect the Pod and set the options in iTunes.

▶ **Microsoft Entourage (Mac)** It's possible to sync your Entourage contacts and calendars with Mac Address Book and iCal, from where iTunes can copy them to your iPod (see above).

▶ **Google contacts & calendars** If you have a click-wheel iPod then you will need to search online for a means of syncing your Google contacts and calendars with one of the programs mentioned above. If you have an iPod touch, iTunes offers a sync option for contacts, but not calendars. You can, however, manage both using Google Sync (google.com/mobile/apple/sync.html).

▶ **MobileMe** To set up MobileMe to sync with an iPod touch choose Settings > Mail, Contacts, Calendars > Add Account > MobileMe. On a PC you will also need to install the MobileMe control panel within the Windows Control Panel if you want MobileMe to sync with contacts and calendars applications on your computer. For a detailed tutorial of how this all works, visit apple.com/mobileme/setup.

▶**Yahoo! contacts** As with Google, click-wheel iPods require you to first sync with one of the default iTunes compatible applications mentioned opposite. iPod touch users, however, are offered a Yahoo! contacts sync option within iTunes.

...and on the iPod

Once all this information is safely aboard your Pod, you'll find it within the Extras menu (on a click-wheel model) or by tapping the Calendar and Contacts icons on the Home screen of an iPod touch. Note that if you've assigned any reminder alerts to calendar events on your Mac or PC, the iPod will beep and/or display an on-screen message at the appropriate time.

Emails

Having email available wherever you are completely changes your relationship with it. It becomes more like text messaging – but much better. As this section explains, the iPod touch makes it possible to send and receive email whenever and wherever you can get online. For other iPod models, the best you can do is sync recent emails for reading when you're away from your computer (see p.201).

Setting up an account

The iPod touch comes preconfig-ured to work with email accounts from AOL, Gmail (aka Google Mail), MobileMe Microsoft Exchange serv-ers and Yahoo!. To set up one of these accounts on the touch itself, just tap Settings > Mail > Add Account..., choose your account provider from the list and enter your normal log-in

Email jargon buster

Email can be collected and sent in various ways, the most common being POP, IMAP and Exchange – all of which are supported by the iPod touch. If you're using an account from your ISP, you may find you can choose between IMAP and POP. Here's the lowdown on each type:

▶ **POP** (or **POP3**) email accounts can be sent and received via an email program such as Mail or Outlook. Each time you check your mail, new messages are downloaded from your provider's mail server onto your computer or phone. It's a bit like a real-world postal service – and, indeed, POP stands for Post Office Protocol. When using a computer, messages are usually deleted from the server as you download them, but it is possible to leave copies on the server so you can download them from other computers. By default, the iPod doesn't delete the messages as it downloads them.

▶ **IMAP** An IMAP account can also be sent and received via an email program, but all the messages are based on your mail provider's server, not on your phone or computer. When you open your mail program, it downloads the email headers (from, to, subject, etc). Clicking on a message will download the full text of the message, but not delete it from the server. This can be a bit slow, but it means your mail archive will be available at all times. It also means the amount of mail you can store will be limited by the server space offered by your provider. IMAP stands for Internet Message Access Protocol.

▶ **Exchange** Exchange is Microsoft's corporate system. If you use Outlook at work, it's likely that you're using an Exchange email account.

▶ **Web access** Most POP, IMAP and Exchange email providers also let you send and receive email via a website. You can access your mail this way on the iPod touch via Safari, though it's much more convenient to use Mail.

details. You may be prompted to log in to your account on the web and enable either POP3 or IMAP access (see box above). You can do this via Safari on your iPod touch, or using a computer.

Setting up other email accounts

If you are using a compatible email application on your PC or Mac, you can sync mail account settings to an iPod touch via iTunes. Connect your Pod and look under the Info tab of the iPod options panel to see if your email application is supported. If it isn't, then you need to return to the iPod touch and enter the settings for your email account manually.

Setting up an email account manually

On the touch, tap Settings > Mail > Add Account… > Other, and choose from IMAP, POP or Exchange. If you're not sure, try POP, or contact your email provider to see what flavour they offer. Fill in the details. If you're not sure and your email address is, say, joebloggs@myisp.com, the username may be joebloggs (or your full email address), the incoming server may be mail.myisp.com or pop.myisp.com; and your outgoing server may be smtp.myisp.com. Press Save when you're done.

Sending and receiving

Using email on the iPod touch works just as you'd expect. Tap Mail on the Home screen, and then…

▶ **Compose a message**
Tap ☑. (If you have more than one account set up, first select the account you want to use from the list.) Alternatively, you can kick-start a message by tapping a name in Contacts and then tapping the contact's email address.

▶ **View a message** Tap any email listed in your Inbox to view the entire message. Double-tap and "pinch" respectively – just like with Safari. If you find that you have to zoom in to read the text, try raising the minimum font size under Settings > Mail, Contacts, Calendars.

▶ **Open an attachment** You can open Word, Excel, PowerPoint, PDF and iWork files attached to emails. You can also view images and save them to Photos to be synced across to your computer. Tap the image in question and choose Save Photo.

▶ **Reply or forward** Open a message and tap ↰.

▶ **Deleting messages** You can delete individual messages by swiping left or right over the message and then tapping Delete. To delete multiple messages simultaneously, tap Edit and check each of the messages you want to trash. Then click the Delete button.

> # TIP:
> A third way to delete messages is to open them and press 🗑. This is convenient as you then jump to the next message. If you delete a lot of messages this way, and you don't want to waste time confirming each time you hit delete, use the slider at Settings > Mail, Contacts, Calendars > Ask Before Deleting.

Push mail versus Fetch mail

Traditionally, a computer or phone only receives new emails when its mail application contacts the relevant server and "fetches" any new messages. On a computer, this happens automatically every few minutes – and whenever you click the Check Mail or Send/Receive button. On the iPod touch, it happens at regular intervals (tap Settings > Fetch New Data to set how frequently) and also when you tap the Mail icon.

By contrast, email accounts that support the "Push" system feed messages to the iPod touch the moment they arrive on the server – which is usually just seconds after your correspondent clicks the send button. Ask your email provider whether they offer push services that are compatible with an iPod touch and, if they do, enable the feature under Settings > Fetch New Data. Of course, push services only really count for anything if your Pod spends the best part of its life connected to Wi-Fi networks and the Internet.

▶ **Moving messages**
To move one or more
messages to a different
folder, hit Edit, check the messages and tap Move. Or, when viewing an
individual message, tap the 📁 button.

▶ **To attach a photo** You can't add an attachment to a message
that you have already started, but you can tap Photos on the Home
screen, select an image, and tap 📤. Next tap Email Photo and type an
accompanying message in the normal way. If you have multiple email
accounts, the message will be sent from the default account, which you
can select under Settings > Mail, Contacts, Calendars.

▶ **Empty the Trash** Each email account offers a Trash folder. When
viewing the contents of the Trash, you can permanently delete individual
items in the normal way. Alternatively, tap Settings > Mail, Contacts,
Calendars, choose an account, and then tap Advanced > Remove and
choose to have messages in the Trash automatically deleted either
never, or after a day, a week, or a month.

> **TIP:** As with Safari, you can tap and hold a link in
> an email to reveal the full destination address.
> Useful for links in emails that seem a bit dodgy.

Tweaking the settings

Once your email account is up and running on your phone, scan
through the Settings options to see what suits you. Some things to
consider:

▶ **Message preview** If you'd like to be able to see more of each
message without clicking it, press Settings > Email > Preview and
increase the number of lines.

▶ **To/Cc** If you'd like to be able to see at a glance whether you were
included in the To: or Cc: field of an email, tap Settings > Mail > Show

To/Cc Label. A small icon will appear by each message preview stating "to" or "cc".

▶ **Sent mail** With a standard email account, messages sent from your iPod touch won't get transferred to the Sent folder on your Mac or PC. If this bothers you, as you'd like to have a complete archive of your mail on your computer, turn on Always CC Myself under Settings > Mail. The downside is that every message you send will pop up in your iPod's inbox a few minutes later. The upside is that you'll get a copy of your sent messages next time you check your

iPod 🛜	8:11 AM	
Settings	Mail, Contacts, Calend...	
Accounts		
My Gmail Account Mail		>
Add Account...		>
Mail		
Show	50 Recent Messages	>
Preview	2 Lines	>
Minimum Font Size	Medium	>
Show To/Cc Label	ON	
Ask Before Deleting	OFF	

mail on your Mac and PC. You can copy these into your Sent folder manually, or set up a rule or filter to do it automatically.

▶ **Default account** If you have more than one email account set up on your iPod, you can choose one to be the default account. This will be used whenever you create messages from other applications – such as when you email a picture from within Photos. So choose the account that you're most likely to use in this way, which might not necessarily be the one you use the most.

▶ **Adding a signature** Even if you have a sign-off signature (name, contact details, etc) set up at home, it won't show up automatically when you use the same account from your iPod touch. To set up a mail signature for your iPod, tap Settings > Mail, Contacts, Calendars > Signature and then enter your signature.

Email problems

You can receive but not send

If you're using an account from your Internet Service Provider, you might find that you can receive emails on the iPod but not send them. If you entered the details manually, go back and check that you inputted the outgoing mail server details correctly, and that your log-in details are right.

If that doesn't work, contact your ISP and ask them if they have an outgoing server address that can be accessed from anywhere, or if they can recommend a "port" for mobile access. If they can, add this number, after a colon, onto the name of your outgoing mail server. For example, if your server is smtp.myisp.com and the port number is 138, enter smtp.att.yahoo.com:138.

You might also try turning on or off the Use SSL option under Settings> Mail, Contacts, Calendars, to see if that makes any difference.

Messages don't arrive unless I check for them

Unless you use a push mail system (see p.198), this is the default setting. If you'd rather have your iPod check for mail automatically, look at your "Fetch" settings (see p.198).

Click-wheel options

If you are determined to transfer unread emails to a click-wheel iPod, even though you won't be able to reply to them, check out one of the following third-party applications:

iPodSync ipod-sync.com (PC)
Jax joesoft.com/products/jax.php (Mac)
Pocket Mac pocketmac.net (Mac)

iPod clock and alarm

To access the various clock and alarm features, select Extras > Clock (on a click-wheel iPod) or tap the Clock icon (on an iPod touch).

▶**World Clock** Click **+** or Edit on an iPod touch, or New Clock on a click-wheel iPod to add and remove locations. Cities where it's currently light will appear with a white clock-face; those where it's dark will appear in black. With an iPod touch you can also reorder the list by tapping Edit and then dragging the ☰ icons.

▶**Alarm Clock** Click-wheel iPods allow you to set one alarm at a time, while the iPod touch lets you set as many as you like: tap the **+** button to create one. Each alarm can be customized with a label and alarm sound and set to repeat on certain days of the week. You can turn individual alarms on or off in the list as you need them.

On any iPod you can choose to be woken by either a preset sound or a playlist of your choice. But unless you like to sleep wearing a pair of headphones, or you have an iPod touch with a built-in speaker, this will rely on you having your iPod hooked up to a hi-fi (see p.177) or speaker system (see p.232).

▶**Stopwatch and Timer** As you'd expect, the Stopwatch (under Extras on click-wheel iPods) counts up, while the Timer (iPod touch only) counts down.

> **TIP:** If you want to double-check that your iPod touch has the correct time, tap Safari and visit onlineclock.net

22

Notes, books & maps

The iPod reader

One of the most useful non-music features found on click-wheel iPods is Notes, which allows you to read text documents when out and about – anything from news stories and travel directions to essay drafts. You can make your own Notes, download them from the Web or even have a program automatically add up-to-date newsfeeds to your iPod each time you sync. The iPod touch gives you even more options, through hundreds of apps (see p.119) that give you access to newsfeeds, academic articles, sample chapters from new books and even entire novels … often for free.

Notes

Also known as PodBooks, Notes are simple-text files (text documents with no formatting) that reside within a special folder on most click-wheel iPod models. To access this folder, first enable your iPod for disk use (see p.190). Then open the iPod drive in Windows or Mac OS X and locate the Notes folder.

Any simple-text doc placed in here can be read on the Pod by browsing Extras > Notes. To delete text docs from your iPod, simply drag them to the Trash (Mac) or Recycle Bin (PC).

Creating your own Notes

All word processors can create and re-save copies of docs in simple text (or "text only") format. Note that if the resulting file is any bigger than 4k (roughly 4000 characters), you'll have to chop it up into smaller chunks in order to make it readable on the iPod.

It is also possible to include links within your Notes – to kick-start an audio track, display a photo or open another Note, for example. This is done with HTML, the code used in webpages.

It's even possible to put the iPod into "NotesOnly" or "Museum" mode, which temporarily locks all other iPod functions. The aim is to allow museums to use iPods for audio tours triggered via Notes. For full details on advanced Notes functions, visit:

Macworld macworld.com/2004/09/secrets/septgeekfactor

Downloading Notes

Take a look online and you'll find iPod-friendly versions of everything from the best of the Bard to health-food recipes:

Shakespeare Sonnets westering.com/ipod
Vegan recipes enriquequinterodesign.com

iSpeak

If you have a Mac, and fancy having Notes read out to you, turn to iSpeak It, which can turn written documents into spoken-word AAC files and inject them into your iTunes collection. It also features links to convert Google News, weather forecasts and the text from any webpage into a similar speech file, all ready for you to take out and about on your Pod.

iSpeak It zapptek.com/ispeak-it

The iPod touch, meanwhile, has its own, self-explanatory note-taking application built-in. The best way to read text documents (even Word docs and PDFs) is to either email them to yourself and then open those attachments on the Pod, or store and view them using a Wi-Fi file storage app from the App Store. We recommend:

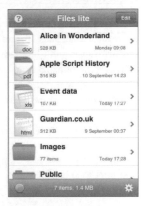

▶ **Files lite (free)** Store and view all manner of files on the touch. The free "lite" version has a capped capacity of 200MB, which is fine for general use. Find out more at olivetoast.com.

Newsfeeds

For click-wheel iPod users there are several applications that will convert RSS newsfeeds into Notes form. This can be great for keeping up to date with news, blogs and other websites. Jax and iPodSync, described on p.238, can handle RSS, though often you'll only get a headline and one-sentence summary for each article. iPod touch users, meanwhile, have a lot more choice. The App

Store features hundreds of RSS feed
managers as well as publication-
specific apps from the likes of the
New York Times, BBC, Associated
Press, *Wall Street Journal*, etc. Browse
the News category of the App Store
for the full choice, though our recommended feed aggregator is the
impressive NetNews Wire:

▶ **NetNews Wire (free)** A news
aggregator that pulls stories from your
favourite sites and RSS feeds. As long
as you remember to sync over Wi-Fi
before heading out the door, you'll have
fresh news to read on your morning commute.

Audiobooks

When it comes to spoken-word content, the most obvious point of call for iPod
owners is the Audiobook section of the iTunes Store. It offers thousands of titles
– from language primers to classic recordings of great novels made by famous
actors – and works in just the same way as the rest of the Store (see Chapter 9).

Also worth exploring is Audible. It has a bigger range than iTunes (tens of thousands of titles) and offers various membership plans that can work out as good
value for regular audiobook purchasers. Audiobooks from Audible and iTunes are
stored in the Audible format (.aa). This means that when you stop or pause while
listening on your iPod or computer, a "bookmark" will be added at that point.
When you return to the audiobook, it will start where you left off.

Audible audible.com

Not that audiobooks necessarily have to cost anything at all. Search online and
you'll come across thousands of freebies, served up by sites such as:

Audiobooks For Free audiobooksforfree.com
Telltale Weekly telltaleweekly.org

Books

Though you could, in theory, chop the text of a novel up into Notes for a click-wheel iPod, the screens are not really that suited for extended reading … you'll probably have more fun with an audiobook (see below). The iPod touch, however, makes a surprisingly satisfactory eBook reader. The App Store is bulging at the seams with individual books that have been converted into apps, but there are also several apps that let you build a personal library of digital

tomes and download fresh titles over Wi-Fi from an online list:

▶ **Classics (99¢/59p)** An ever expanding list of classic fiction in a beautifully presented reader.

▶ **Penguin US (free)** The latest news, blogs, interviews, excerpts and whole books from Penguin.

▶ **Stanza (free)** Another extensive collection of titles, this time with a pleasing Cover Flow-like interface.

Maps

The Maps widget on the iPod touch takes you into the world of Google Maps, where you can quickly find locations, get directions and even view satellite photos. You can zoom and scroll around the maps in the same way you would with webpages in Safari, double-tapping or "pinching" to zoom in and out. You need to be connected to a Wi-Fi network to fetch the map data from the Internet.

Searching for yourself

Though the iPod touch does not have built-in GPS (like the iPhone), it can cleverly have a stab at determining your location based on nearby Wi-Fi networks. To do this, connect to a network and then tap the ○ icon in the Maps widget.

Searching for locations

Tap the Search box and type a city, town or region, place of interest, or a ZIP code or postcode. You can also try to find a business in the area you are viewing by tapping the search box and entering either the name of the business or something more general – such as "camera", "hotel", or "pizza". Note, however, that the results, which are pulled from Google Local, won't be comprehensive.

Search results appear as a little red pin. Tap the pin's ❷ button for further options such as adding the location as a bookmark or contact address, or getting the directions to or from that location.

Dropping pins

You can also drop a pin manually at any time by tapping the curled page icon and then Drop Pin. This can be handy to keep your bearings when sliding around a map. To change the position

> **TIP:** To toggle between regular maps, satellite views, and a "hybrid" of the two, tap the curled page icon and make your selection.

of a pin, press and hold it and drag it to a
correct location. To delete the pin, add it
as a bookmark for future reference, or get
directions to and from the location, tap
the pin and use the ❷ button. Your lists of
bookmarks and recently viewed locations
can be viewed by tapping the 🕮 button,
which appears in the right of the search
field when it is empty.

Directions

To view driving directions between two
locations, tap Directions at the bottom of the screen and enter
start and end points, either by typing search terms or by tapping 🕮 to browse for bookmarks, recently viewed locations and
addresses from your Contacts. When you're done, tap Route.

> **TIP:** For your return journey, reverse the directions
> given by your iPod by tapping the ↻ button.

Traffic conditions

In areas where the service is available, your journey's route will
display colour-coded information about traffic conditions. The
approximate driving time at the top of the screen will change to
take account of the expected traffic conditions:

► **Grey** No data currently available

► **Red** Traffic moving at less than 25 miles per hour

►**Yellow** Traffic moving at 25–50 miles per hour

► **Green** Traffic moving at more than 50 miles per hour

If you don't see any change in colour, you may need to zoom out.

More maps

Though Google Maps is probably the single best online map service, it may not always find what you're looking for. So bear in mind that (assuming you are connected to Wi-Fi) you also have the web at your fingertips:

Multimap multimap.com
Transport For London tfl.gov.uk/maps
World Maps justmaps.org

And there are also loads of map and travel apps worth investigating in the App Store. Start with:

▶ **iOSMaps (free)** UK Ordinance Survey in your pocket.

▶ **London Mini A-Z ($9.99/£5.99)** Very handy, and, as the maps are pre-loaded, it even works without a Wi-Fi connection.

Something for the click-wheel

In a similar vein, iSubwayMaps produce full-colour metro maps for cities around the world that work in click-wheel iPods. Like PodScrolls (see below), they are accessed via the Photos menu.

iSubwayMaps isubwaymaps.com

Rough Guides PodScrolls

PodScrolls exploit the photo capabilities of click-wheel colour-screen iPods.

PodScrolls are in full colour, with page numbers, images and more – just like real books, but much quicker to flick through. Rough Guides were the first to exploit this new format, offering eating and drinking guides to ten of the world's great cities.

Rough Guides PodScrolls roughguides.com/podscrolls

23

Wi-Fi &
the Web

Connecting and surfing
with an iPod touch

The iPod touch is the first iPod to offer Web browsing
features. Like the iPhone, it comes with a fully functioning
Web browser – Safari. Unlike the iPhone, however, the iPod
touch can only get online via Wi-Fi, so to connect to the
Internet you'll need to be within range of a Wi-Fi network. This
chapter takes a quick look at managing the Wi-Fi features of an
iPod touch and how to make the most of the Web with a 3.5-
inch screen.

Using Wi-Fi

Connecting to networks

To connect to a Wi-Fi network, tap Settings > Wi-Fi and choose a network from the list. If it's a secure wireless network (as indicated by the padlock icon), you'll be invited to enter the password.

Though this procedure doesn't take long, it's best to have the iPod point you in the direction of Wi-Fi networks automatically. This way, whenever you open an Internet-based tool such as Safari (see p.215), and there are no known networks in range, the iPod will automatically present you with a list of all the networks it can find. You can turn this feature on and off via the Settings > Wi-Fi > Ask to Join Networks toggle switch.

If the network you want to connect to isn't in the list, you could be out of range, or it could be that it's a "hidden" network, in which case tap Wi-Fi > Other and enter its name, password and password type.

> **TIP:** If you want to maximize battery life, get into the habit of turning Wi-Fi off when you're not using it. It only takes a couple of seconds to turn it back on when you next need it.

Finding public hotspots

Many cafés, hotels, airports and other public places offer free wireless Internet access, though often you'll have to pay for the privilege of using them – particularly in establishments which are part of big chains (Starbucks and the like). You either pay the person running the system (over the counter in a café, for instance) or connect and sign up on-screen. If you use such services a lot, you may save time and money by signing up to a service such as Boingo, T-Mobile or Wayport, which allow you to connect at thousands of hotspots for a monthly fee.

Boingo boingo.com
T-Mobile t-mobile.com/hotspot
Wayport wayport.com

The ideal, of course, is to stick to free hotspots. There are various online directories that will help you locate them, though none is comprehensive:

Hotspot Locations hotspot-locations.com
WIFInder wifinder.com
Wi-Fi Free Spot wififreespot.com
ZONE Finder wi-fi.jiwire.com

Forgetting networks

Once you've connected to a Wi-Fi network, the iPod touch will remember it as a trusted network and connect to it automatically whenever you're in range. This is useful but can be annoying – if, for example, the iPod keeps connecting to a network you once chose accidentally. In these cases, click on the ⊘ icon next to the relevant network name and tap Forget This Network. This won't stop you connecting to it manually in the future.

When it won't connect…

If your iPod refuses to connect to a Wi-Fi network, try again, in case you mistyped the password or tapped the wrong network name. If you still have no luck, try the following:

►**Try WEP Hex** If there's a ◉ icon in the password box, tap it, choose WEP Hex and try again.

► **Check the settings** Some networks, especially in offices, require you to manually enter information such as an IP address. Ask your network administrator for the details and plug them in by clicking ◉ next to the relevant network name.

►**Add your MAC address** Some routers in homes and offices (but not in public hotspots) will only allow access to a list of pre-approved devices. If this is the case, you'll need to add the iPod's MAC address – which you'll find within Settings > General > About > Wi-Fi Address – to your router's list. This usually means entering the router's setup screen and looking for something titled MAC Filtering or Access List.

► **Reboot the router** If you're at home, try rebooting your wireless router by turning it off or unplugging it for a few seconds. Turn off the Wi-Fi on the iPod (Settings > Wi-Fi) until the router has rebooted.

►**Tweak your router settings** If the above doesn't work, try temporarily turning off your router's wireless password to see whether that fixes the problem. If it does, try choosing a different type of password (WEP rather than WPA, for example). If that doesn't help, try updating the firmware (internal software) of the router, in case the current version isn't compatible with the iPod's hardware. Check the manufacturer's website to see if a firmware update is available.

Test your speed

To test the speed and latency (time lag) of your current Wi-Fi signal, tap Safari and visit the following site.

Tiny Speed Test i.dslr.net/tinyspeedtest.html

The Web: Safari and more

The iPod touch certainly isn't the first mobile device to offer Web browsing. But arguably it's the first – along with the iPhone – to provide tools that make it a pleasure to use, as opposed to a headache. The iPod touch comes with a nearly fully fledged version of the Safari Web browser. It can't do everything – Flash and Java items won't display, at the time of writing – but it's still hugely impressive.

The basics

Make sure you have a Wi-Fi signal (see p.213) and tap Safari on the Home screen. Then...

▶ **Enter an address** Click at the top of the screen, tap ⊗ to clear the current address and start typing. Note the ".com" key for quickly completing addresses.

▶ **Search Google** Click at the top of the screen, tap in the Google field and start typing. When you're finished, hit Google. If you want to switch from Google to Yahoo! searching, look within Settings > Safari > Search Engine. Of course, you can also visit any search engine manually and use it in the normal way.

▶ **To follow a link** Tap once. If you did it by accident, press ✕.

▶ **Reload/refresh** If a page hasn't loaded properly, or you want to make sure you're viewing the latest version of the page, click ↻.

▶ **Zoom** Double-tap on any part of a page – a column, headline or

> **TIP:** You can see the full URL of any link by tapping and holding the relevant text or image. (This is equivalent to hovering over a link with a mouse and looking at the status bar at the bottom of a normal Web browser.)

picture, say – to zoom in on it or zoom back out. Alternatively, "pinch" with your finger and thumb (or any two digits of your choice): pull your digits together to zoom out and move them apart to zoom in. Once zoomed, you can drag the page around with one finger.

Multiple pages

Just like a browser on a Mac or PC, Safari on the iPod touch can handle multiple pages at once. These are especially useful when you're struggling with a slow Wi-Fi network, and you don't want to close a page that you may want to come back to later. The only pain is that you can't tap a link and ask it to open in a new window.

▶ **Open a new page** Tap ⬚ then New Page.

▶ **Switch between pages** Tap ⬚ and flick left or right. To close a page, tap ❸.

History & cache

Like most browsers, Safari on the iPod touch stores a list of all the websites you visit. These allow the iPod to offer suggestions when you're typing an address but can also be browsed – useful if you need to find a site for the second time but can't remember its address. To browse your history, look at the top of your Bookmarks list, accessible at any time via the ⌗ icon. To clear your history, look for the option in Settings > Safari.

Unfortunately, despite storing your history, Safari doesn't "cache" (temporarily save) each page you visit in any useful way. This is a shame, as it means you can't quickly visit a bunch of pages for browsing when you've got no Wi-Fi reception. It also explains why using the Back button is slower on the iPod touch than on a computer – when you click ◀, you download the page in question afresh rather than returning to a cached version.

Opening links in new windows

The multiple webpages function is great. Annoyingly, however, the iPod touch doesn't offer a way to open a link on the current page in a new window. To get around this, grab Richard Herrera's (doctyper.com) clever little bookmarklet, which allows you to make all links on any page open in a new window simply by clicking a special bookmark entry.

Bookmarks

Bookmarks are always handy, but when using a device without a mouse and keyboard, they're even handier than usual.

The basics

To bookmark a page to return to later on the iPod touch, click **+**. To retrieve a bookmark, tap ⌗, browse and then click the relevant entry. It's also possible to edit your bookmarks list on the iPod:

▶**To delete a bookmark or folder** Tap Edit followed by the relevant ● icon. Hit delete to confirm.

▶**To edit a bookmark or folder** Tap Edit, then hit the relevant entry and type into the name and URL fields.

▶**To move a bookmark or folder** Tap Edit and slide it up or down using the ≡ icon. Alternatively, tap Edit, then hit the relevant entry and use the third option down to pick the folder you'd like to move the bookmark or folder into.

> **TIP:** If you struggle with the on-screen keyboard, try rotating the iPod when typing in Safari: the landscape mode offers bigger keys.

Importing bookmarks from your Mac or PC

iTunes lets you quickly transfer bookmarks from a Mac or PC to your iPod touch. Just connect your iPod and click its icon in iTunes. Under the Info tab, check the relevant box under Web Browser. The bookmarks will move across to the iPod, though they can be easy to miss: if you use Safari on your Mac or PC, you'll find them within two folders labelled Bookmarks Menu and Bookmarks Toolbar.

Likewise, bookmarks from the iPod will appear back in your browser. In Safari, you won't find them in the Bookmarks menu, however: you'll have to click Show All Bookmarks or the 🕮 icon.

Importing Firefox bookmarks

At the time of writing, the iPod touch only syncs bookmarks with Safari or Internet Explorer – not Firefox. However, it is perfectly possible to get your Firefox bookmarks onto your Pod via either Safari or Explorer.

By far the easiest way to keep your Firefox bookmarks in sync with either Safari or Internet Explorer is the free add-on Xmarks. It works slightly differently for each browser, so check out the website for the full story:

Xmarks xmarks.com

Because Xmarks syncs in both directions, it also means that any new bookmarks that you create on the iPod will in turn end up back on each of your browsers, and even across multiple computers if they are all hooked in with the same Xmarks account.

> **TIP:** Xmarks also makes your bookmarks available online at my.xmarks.com, accessible from any desktop or mobile browser.

Other browsing tips

Searching for text on a page

One very useful tool currently missing from the iPod touch version of Safari is the ability to search for text within a page. This is especially annoying when you follow a link in Google and end up on a very long page with no idea where your search terms appear.

To circumvent this, get into the habit, when searching the Web, of visiting Google's "cached" (saved and indexed) version of a webpage rather than the "live" version. You'll find a link for this option next to each of the results when you search Google. Click "Cached" and see a version of the target page that's got each of your search terms highlighted in a different colour throughout – almost as good as being able to click Find.

Rough Guides Travel
travel and music guide publishers; includes an online guide to destinations throughout the world,...
www.**roughguides**.com/ - 24k - Cached - Similar pages

Webpage display problems

If a webpage looks weird on screen – bad spacing, images overlapping, etc – there are two likely causes. First, it could be that the page isn't properly "Web compliant". That is, it looks OK on the browser the designer tested it on (Internet Explorer, for example), but not on other browsers (such as Safari or Firefox). The solution is to try viewing the page through another browser.

Second, it could be that the page includes elements based on technologies that the iPod touch doesn't yet handle, such as Flash, Real and Windows Media. This is especially likely to be the problem if there's a gap in an otherwise normal page.

If a webpage looks OK, but different from the version you're used to seeing on your Mac or PC, it could be that the website in question has been set up to detect your browser and automatically offer you a small-screen version.

iPod Googling tips

Given that your connection speed may sometimes be slow, and because you don't have access to Google Toolbar and the like, it makes sense to hone your search skills for use on the iPod touch. All the following tricks work on a PC or Mac, too.

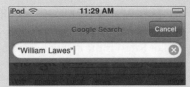

Basic searches

All these commands can be mixed and doubled up. Hence:

Googling this...	*Finds pages containing...*
william lawes	the terms "william" and "lawes"
"william lawes"	the phrase "william lawes"
william OR lawes	either "william", "lawes" or both
william -lawes	"william" but not "lawes"
"william lawes" OR "will lawes" -composer	*either* version of the name but not the word "composer"

Synonyms

~mac	"mac" and related words, such as "Apple" and "macintosh"

Definitions

define:calabash	definitions from various sources for the word "calabash". You can also get definitions of a search term from answers. com by clicking the link in the right of the top blue strip on the results page.

Flexible phrases

| "william * lawes" | "william john lawes" as well as just "william lawes" |

Search within a specific site

| site:bbc.co.uk "jimmy white" | pages containing Jimmy White's name within the BBC website. This is often far more effective than using a site's internal search. |

Search Web addresses

| "arms exports" inurl:gov | the phrase "arms exports" in webpages with the term gov in the address (ie government websites) |

Search page titles

| train bristol intitle:timetable | pages with "timetable" in their titles, and "train" and "bristol" anywhere in the page |

Number & price ranges

| 1972..1975 "snooker champions" | the term "snooker champions" and any number (or date) in the range 1972–1975 |
| $15..$30 "snooker cue" | the term "snooker cue" and any price in the range $15–30 |

Search specific file types

| filetype:pdf climate change statistics | would find pdf documents (likely to be more "serious" reports than webpages) containing the terms "climate", "change" and "statistics" |

Safari options

You'll find various browsing preferences under Settings > Safari. Here you can empty your cache and history (useful if Safari keeps crashing, or you want to hide your tracks), and turn the following on or off:

▶ **Javascript**: a ubiquitous way to add extra functions to websites.

▶ **Pop-up blocker**: stops pop-up pages (mainly ads) from opening.

▶ **Cookies**: files that websites save on your iPod to allow customizations such as "we recommend".

Viewing online PDFs and Word documents

The iPod touch's browser *can* view Word, Excel and PDF documents on the Web, but it can take quite a while for them to appear, as they have to be downloaded and turned into an iPod-friendly preview version before anything is displayed.

So… be patient. Or, if you can't be patient, and you're following a link from Google to a PDF, Word or Excel doc, click the "View As HTML" link instead of the main link to the document. This way you'll get a faster-loading text-only version.

Webpages optimized for the iPod touch

Though the iPod touch and iPhone can handle almost all webpages, some are specially designed to work perfectly on their small screens, with no zooming required. The best way to find them is to use one of the following directories. Add them to your iPod's bookmarks for quick access:

iLounge ilounge.com/index.php/mobile/iphonecats
iPhone Apps Manager iphoneappsmanager.com

24

Accessories

Plug and play

There are scores of iPod accessories available. There are the obvious items, such as cases, where you are simply striking a balance between functionality and looks – if you want it waterproof, visit over-board.co.uk and for something seriously protective otterboxshop.com. Then there are the less obvious items, such as solar chargers and integrated car audio systems. The following pages show some of the most useful and desirable add-ons available, but new ones come out all the time, so keep an eye on iPod news sites (see p.262). When it comes to purchasing, some accessories can be bought on the high street, but for the best selection and prices look online. Compare the offerings of the Apple Store, Amazon, eBay and others, or go straight to the manufacturers, many of whom sell direct. Before buying any accessory, make sure it is compatible with the iPod model you own.

Voice recorders

Models include: Belkin TuneTalk; Belkin Universal Microphone Adapter
Cost (approx): $30–70/£20–40

Journalists, writers and thinkers who want to be able to record interviews or thoughts on the move will welcome the opportunity to turn their iPod into a Dictaphone capable of recording hundreds – even thousands – of hours of audio. Voice recorders let you do just this. They generally plug into the Dock socket, providing a built-in microphone and, often, a socket for an external mic as well.

Some models, such as the TuneTalk (pictured below), can even record in true stereo thanks to directional mics. Once you're done, the sounds are saved, ready for transfer to a computer for storage, compressing, emailing or editing.

If you want more control over the recording level, get the Belkin Universal Microphone Adapter, which has a variable gain switch. The sound quality of such devices is impressive, but not perfect.

iPod touch voice recorder apps

The iPod touch has no built-in microphone, but it will work with earphones that do, allowing you to do things such as make Skype calls (see p.122) or record audio. Once you have the hardware, recording can be made possible using one of many apps from the App Store. Try one of these:

Record - Voice Recorder 99¢/59p
Audio Memos Free free
FourTrack $9.99/£5.99

Battery packs & charging

Models include: Griffin TuneJuice2; Belkin TunePower Rechargable;
FreeLoader Solar Charger
Cost (approx): $60/£40

If you find the iPod's
battery doesn't last long
enough, an external bat-
tery pack will allow you to
keep the music playing for
longer. The Griffin model,
pictured, attaches to the
Pod via the Dock socket
and takes four standard
AAA batteries.

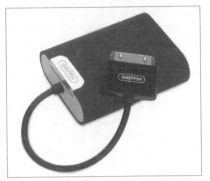

Battery packs do exactly
what they say on the tin,
but if you mainly use your iPod in the car, you'll get better value
from an in-car power cable (see p.229).

A more sustainable option would be an iPod solar charger such as
the FreeLoader (freeloader.com.au). Again, this gadget connects via

the Dock socket and can
be used in even relatively
low light conditions to
slowly trickle charge your
Pod back to full strength
– great for camping trips.
It comes with a plethora
of adapters, so can be used
with other devices too.

FM radio transmitters

Models include: Belkin TuneCast; Griffin iTrip; XtremeMac AirPlay
Cost (approx): $40–60

These cunning little devices turn an iPod into an extremely short-range FM radio station. (Many will also work with a computer or any other device with a headphone jack, though check before buying.) Once you've attached a transmitter to your iPod, any radio within range – theoretically around thirty feet, though a few feet is more realistic to achieve decent sound – can tune in to whatever the Pod is playing.

The sound quality isn't as good as you'd get via a cable and there can be interference, especially in cities. But FM transmitters are very convenient and allow you to play through any FM radio, including those – such as portables and car stereos – which don't offer a line-in.

Of the models available at the time of writing, the iTrip (pictured), which is available in black or white, has the advantage of taking power directly from the Pod, so no batteries are required and there are no annoying cables. However, some users have complained of a weak signal compared to other models such as the Belkin TuneCast, which takes two AAA batteries or plugs into the mains or a car socket.

FM transmitters have always been legal in North America but until recently they couldn't be sold in Europe due to radio transmission laws. Thanks to a change to the Wireless Telegraphy Act, however, they've been legal since December 2006.

Cables & connections

TV connection cables

Models include: The Monster iTV Link; Apple iPod AV Cable
Cost (approx): $20–40/£15–30

If you want to connect your colour-screen
iPod to a TV, you'll need either an AV
cable or an S-video cable. Apple do
a very "white" AV cable, though
a regular AV to three-striped
minijack will do the trick (see
p.80). To go the S-video
route you'll need the
appropriate Apple Dock
(see p.228) and a cable
such as the Monster iTV
Link (pictured).

Headphone splitters

Models include: splitters by Monster and others
Cost (approx): $10/£5

Headphone splitters allow you to
connect two pairs of headphones
to a single iPod – or any other
device with a minijack socket.

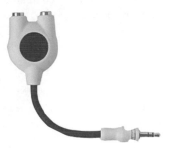

Docks & stands

Models include: Apple iPod Dock; Wadia's iTransport
Cost (approx): $15–350/£10–200

An iPod Dock makes it easy to connect and disconnect your Pod to computers, power sources, hi-fis and TVs. The Dock's various connections can be left permanently in place, so when you get home you simply drop in your Pod and it's instantly hooked up.

Apple's own Universal Dock features a genuine line-out socket – as opposed to a headphone socket – so the sound quality is improved when playing through a hi-fi; you can also use the line-out socket with an appropriate AV cable to view photos or videos on a connected TV. Best of all, the Dock boasts an infrared receiver for the Apple Remote (see p.234). Third-party equivalents tend to be less expensive but aren't all well-made. Whichever brand you choose, be sure to get the right dock or dock adapter for your specific iPod model.

Docks come in all shapes and sizes – with price tags to match. If you have the budget and want to squeeze every last ounce of sound quality out of your iPod, you might consider the iTransport (pictured), which promises markedly superior fidelity compared to many other means of connecting an iPod to a hi-fi or amplifier. It also comes with its own remote control. Visit wadia.com to find out more.

Car accessories

Several car manufacturers offer iPod connectivity options (see apple.com/ipod/carintegration.html for a complete list). But don't worry if you lack a recent high-end vehicle – there are various other options for Podding your ride.

Complete systems

Models include: Alpine head unit and interface
Cost (approx): $350/£250

This is the slickest solution: a car-stereo head unit with a jog wheel for directly controlling your iPod and a screen that lets you browse  and see what's currently playing. Your Pod is safely stowed in the glove compartment, where it is charged by the car's battery.

Cassette adapters

If you don't want the expense and hassle of replacing your car stereo system, try a cassette adapter or an FM transmitter (see p.226). Either way, the sound quality, though not perfect, should be good enough for in-car use – especially with models such as Griffin's SmartDeck, which also lets you control the iPod using the buttons of the car's cassette player.

Also available are power cables for recharging via a cigar-lighter socket, and "holsters" – essentially in-car docks, some of which have power connections and FM transmitters built in. For more auto iPod solutions visit:

iPod Car Kit Direct (UK) ipodcarkitdirect.co.uk
MP3 Your Car (US) mp3yourcar.com

Travel speakers

Models include: iHome iHM77 Stereo Mini Speakers; Logitech Pure-Fi
Anywhere Speakers
Cost (approx): $50–130/£30–100

If you travel with your iPod, a
small pair of speakers is great
to have. Any powered speakers
with a line-in or minijack cable
will do the job, including those
used for computers. However,
there are many iPod-specific
models available, complete with
Dock connectors. Some will
also charge your iPod whilst
they play – very handy feature

when away from home for a week or two.

Speakers with their own power source (battery or plug) let the
music play longer and louder than those which draw their energy
from the iPod. Our favourites are those by iHome (pictured
above), which pleasingly and practically fold away into a bullet-
like shape, and the Logitech Anywhere Speakers (pictured below),
which have a fantastic sound for their size.

Earphones

The "earbuds" that come with iPods are not exactly hi-fi, they do tend to get fried quite quickly and they have a very annoying habit of leaking music, as anyone who regularly uses public transport will no doubt be aware. And on top of all that it's quite hard to get them to stay in your ears in the first place. There are thousands of alternatives you could consider (you'll find reviews of loads at headphone.com), but the type that are really worth checking out – since you probably use your iPod when out and about in noisy surroundings – are sound-isolating in-ear headphones.

In-ear headphones

Models include: Apple In-Ear Headphones; Shure SF; Etymotic hf
Cost (approx): $79+/£54+

This kind of earphone sticks into the ear canal, in the process removing much ambient sound. The sound is much improved as a result – and you can listen to music at much lower volume levels, too, which is better for your ears. There are some relatively inexpensive models on the market, including Apple's own In-Ear head-phones that feature a mic and remote halfway along the cord. If you can afford a bit more, check out the models from Shure (store.shure.com) – a company which made its name manufacturing microphones. The isolation is impressive and the sound even more so. If you have money to burn, another manufacturer worth investi-gating is Etymotic. Their hf-series headphones produce a stunning sound (etymotic.com).

Home speaker units

Models include: SoundDock by Bose; Logic3 IP104 Speakers; Apple Hi-Fi
Cost (approx): $50–350

An alternative to connecting your iPod to a hi-fi or powered speakers is a self-contained speaker system. These are easy to move from room to room (or indeed, from place to place when travelling) and they're space efficient too. A long-standing favourite with iPod owners is the Bose SoundDock. At $300, it's not cheap, but the sound is exceptionally clear and punchy for the size.

Apple's own home-speaker unit, the Apple Hi-Fi, costs even more (in the US at least), but offers a line input so you can hook up a CD or DVD player, AirPort Express or any other audio device. And if you don't mind buying enough batteries to power a small village, it can be taken out and about ghettoblaster-style. It works fine with all recent iPod models, but you will need to get hold of the right dock adapter to plug in.

There are many smaller, less expensive systems available. One example is the Logic3 IP104, which can hold an iPod touch in either portrait or land-scape mode, giving you access to Cover Flow and video playback.

Powered speakers

Models include: Audioengine 5; Genelec 8030A
Cost (approx): $350–1200

One problem with the iPod speaker units described opposite is that they offer no flexibility in terms of stereo separation – unlike traditional hi-fi speakers, which you can position as far apart as you like. Pairs of powered speakers – aka active speakers – get around this problem. One or both of the speakers contains its own amplifier, so all you need is a sound source – such as an iPod or your computer.

The Audioengine 5 stands out as a very neat solution (pictured here with an iPod dock connected). These 70W-per-channel speakers feature a USB port up-top for charging and a separate minijack socket for the audio. For the price ($250), they sound excellent.

At the top end of the market are Genelec's range of bi-amplified speakers (that is both speakers have an integrated amplifier). These have long been a popular choice for studio use, thanks to their incredibly detailed and rich sound, but they're equally well suited for audiophile home use. Each speaker connects using its own XLR cable, so you'll have to get a suitable two-channel preamp or DI box to create a "balanced" signal from your iPod. The resulting sound is hugely impressive.

chapter 24

Wireless remotes

Models include: Apple Remote; Griffin AirClick
Cost (approx): $29–50/£19–35

If you (a) play your iPod through your hi-fi or TV, and (b) don't like getting out of your chair, you'll like the idea of a wireless iPod remote control. Obviously, it won't allow you to browse, but it will let you access volume, play/pause and previous/next controls from anywhere in the room – or even further afield.

For home use, the ideal option is to buy an Apple Universal Dock (see p.228) which comes with an Apple Remote (pictured). Apple Remotes also come with new Macs, which can be controlled with the same unit.

Alternatively, try a third-party product such as the Griffin AirClick (pictured). Because they don't require the Dock to function, these can be useful on the move and in the car. The disadvantage is that you can't recharge your Pod or connect to a Dock while using an AirClick with a recent iPod, as your Pod's Dock connector is already occupied by the receiver unit.

The AirClick USB version connects to your computer to offer remote control of iTunes and various other applications.

If you have an iPod touch you can go one better, and control iTunes using Apple's Remote app (see p.241).

AirClick

234

25

Extra software

iPod and iTunes self-improvement

I f you've ever browsed a software download website and seen the amazing quantity of free and nearly free booty on offer, you won't be surprised to learn that there are scores of extra applications, utilities and plug-ins available for use with iTunes and the iPod. We've spotlighted a few useful or interesting things in the next few pages, but there are loads more to be found throughout this book, and on the websites listed on p.260. If you are an iPod touch user, the sky really is the limit and you should turn to p.119 to find out about the App Store.

iPod-iTunes copying tools

Platform: Mac & PC
Cost: Shareware

There are a number of programs available that will let you copy music from your iPod to a computer – very useful if you want to restore your iTunes Library in the event of your computer dying or being stolen, or if you upgrade to a new machine. You could also use one of these applications to donate the music on your iPod to your friends, though doing so with copyrighted music files may push you on to the wrong side of the law.

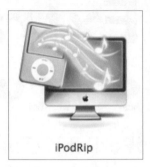

iPodRip

iPod.iTunes and iPodRip will do the job on a Mac, while CopyTrans3 is a good choice for PC users.

iPod.iTunes crispsofties.com
iPodRip thelittleappfactory.com
CopyTrans3 copytrans.net

These kinds of applications can also help you perform other syncing tasks with an iPod and iTunes, though they sometimes stop working when you install a new version of iTunes or update your iPod's software. In this instance, check the developer's website to download the latest version.

AppleScripts & Actions

Platform: Mac
Cost: Freeware

AppleScript is a simple programming language that can be used to automate tasks and functions on a Mac. And if your machine is running OS X Tiger (or later) you also have the option of achieving the same end with the in-built Automator application, which offers a non-techie environment for combining "Actions" to create time-saving "Workflows". Hundreds of AppleScripts and Actions have been written for iTunes and iPods and can be downloaded for free. They can do everything from rearranging track info to making it possible to delete song files directly from a playlist. Start here:

Doug's AppleScripts For iTunes dougscripts.com
Automator Actions apple.com/downloads/macosx/automator

iTunes controllers

Platform: Mac
Cost: Shareware

iTunes controller programs come in many forms and with loads of different features: floating windows, hotkeys, alarm clocks, menu-bar controls, etc. A few worth checking out are M-Beat, SizzlingKeys You Control and MenuTunes; search the download archives listed on p.262 for many more.

M-Beat thelittleappfactory.com
MenuTunes ithinksw.com
SizzlingKeys yellowmug.com/sk4it
You Control yousoftware.com/tunes

Jax & iPodSync

Platform: Mac and PC
Cost: $17–50

Mentioned elsewhere in this book, Jax and iPodSync are tools for automatically loading your click-wheel iPod with all sorts of data. They can keep your Pod up to date with unread email, address book and calendar entries, Notes/Stickies and bookmarks. They can also download RSS feeds for news, weather, stock-market reports, horoscopes and more. Jax can even fetch album artwork and song lyrics for you and then dish up the latest movie listings in your area. These applications can also manage file backups and podcasts. For more information, see:

iPodSync ipod-sync.com (PC)
Jax joesoft.com (Mac)

iPod icons

Platform: Mac (some PC available)
Cost: Free

Anyone who wants to turn their computer into an iPod shrine will be interested in the free icon families – including many devoted to Pods – available from sites such as:

IconFactory iconfactory.com (Mac)
IconArchive iconarchive.com (Mac & PC)

To apply an icon that you've downloaded onto your Mac, select it and press ⌘C (copy). Then select the file or folder on which you want to use it and press ⌘I. Click the current icon at the top of the box and press ⌘V (paste) to overwrite it with the new one; you can get rid of it later by clicking it here and pressing backspace.

If you can't find a Mac icon that does your iPod justice, then download the Pic2Icon app (sugarcubesoftware.com) and make your own.

Hacking the iPod's icons

If you're technically minded and not scared of nullifying your warranty (or even permanently damaging your Pod), you could try customizing the icons, fonts and other elements on your iPod's screen. For the full story, see: *ilounge.com/index.php/articles/comments/beginners-guide-to-changing-ipod-graphics*

Album art grabbers

Platform: Mac or PC
Cost: €30

This book contains a whole chapter on dealing with album artwork in iTunes (see p.156), but there are also third-party applications available for download that can handle the job of fetching
album artwork and associating it with the files in iTunes. The
advantage of such programs is that they give you the control to
choose between possible artwork options, so that you can make
sure that you get exactly the cover you want.

On a Mac, the best option is the Cover Flow-esque CoverScout,
which has a beautiful interface and loads of useful features. If
you run iTunes in Windows, try iAlbumArtwork, which trawls
Amazon for the artwork that's missing from your collection.

CoverScout equinux.com (Mac)
iAlbumArtwork ialbumart.ipod-sync.com (PC)

Remote

Platform: iPod touch, with Mac or PC
Cost: Free

Combined with an iPod touch, Apple's Remote app (free to download from the App Store, see p.119) is a great way to control iTunes across a wireless network. To connect for the first time, make sure that iTunes is running on your computer and then launch Remote on the iPod. Next, tap Settings > Add library. The iPod will then give you a 4-digit code. In iTunes, highlight the Remote icon that will have appeared in the Sources sidebar and then enter the code. If you don't pair your iPod in this way,

you will only be able to connect as an iTunes DJ guest (see p.132) and not directly control any music playback.

Once paired, the controls within Remote appear pretty similar to the iPod's own browse and play controls. Note, however, that when you tap album artwork, you not only get scrubber and Genius controls, but also a strip labelled Speakers, for switching between different sets of remote speakers and the computer's own speakers.

And a few more...

BeaTunes beatunes.com (free trial available)
For Mac and PC, this set of tools analyzes your iTunes library to find typos, multiple artist spellings and the like. It's BPM detection features help you build better playlists.

DJay djay-software.com ($50)
On-screen turntables and DY effects with perfect iTunes integration.

HookUp dotpod.net (free)
Make the songs in your iTunes collection available over the Internet.
Can be very useful, though it's only legal with uncopyrighted music.

iSpazz stewreo.de/keyboarddisco.html (free)
Possibly one of the oddest bits of software you might want to install, iSpazz transforms the backlite keyboard of recent Apple MacBooks into a strobbing, pulsing iTunes visualizer.

LED Spectrum Analyser apptree.net/ledsa.htm (free)
A Mac-only visualizer program that emulates a spectrum analyzer.

Songbird getsongbird.com (free)
An alternative jukebox application that can run alongside iTunes and share its library. Coming from the same stable as Firefox, it has loads of interesting features and an open source community developing new add-ons all the time.

SongGenie equinux.com (€25)
Flawless iTunes labelling and tidying application.

TapeDeck tapedeckapp.com (free trial available)
Nostalgic audio recording tool with iTunes integration.

webRemote deadendsw.com/Products/webRemote.html ($10)
Control iTunes using any Web browser.

First aid

26

Backing up
Keeping your music safe

J ust like any other computer file, music and video files can
be deleted or damaged. Hard drives die, and computers
get stolen, damaged or destroyed. With the right software it's
usually possible to recover music and video from your iPod
back to your computer (see p.236). But then there are all your
apps, photos, emails and settings to consider.
And if you have more music on your
computer than your Pod, or if
you regularly carry your
laptop and Pod around
in the same bag, it's
definitely worth having
a backup copy of your
whole archive.

Back up the iTunes folder

Backing up iTunes properly is not simply a matter of duplicating the song and video files. You also need to back up your iTunes Library file, which stores your playlists, preferences and so on.

Ideally, you should back up to an external medium that you can store separately from your PC or Mac. This way you'll still have it if the computer is ever stolen or the drive damaged. The two obvious choices are external hard drives and CDs/DVDs, each of which are discussed below.

If you *only* want to back up your playlist data, and not the actual song and video files, choose File > Library > Export Library…

Backing up to a hard drive

An external hard drive is the most convenient back-up option. Such drives offer plenty of space, they're easy and quick to use, and they're relatively inexpensive these days.

> **TIP:** If you have a recent AirPort Extreme router and attached hard drive or an Apple Time Capsule, you can back up wireless across your home network using OS X's Time Machine feature.

Getting started

Before backing up to a hard drive, consider running the Consolidate Library tool, which you'll find in the iTunes File > Library menu. This way, iTunes will make sure that everything in your iTunes collection is stored in your iTunes folder. Next, quit iTunes and drag your entire iTunes folder onto your external hard drive. You'll find the iTunes folder here:

▶ **On a Mac** Home Folder > Music > iTunes
▶ **On a PC** My Music > iTunes

Subsequent backups

Whenever you want to update your backup, simply drag the current iTunes folder to your external drive, replacing the previous version if you like. You could, alternatively, use a third-party application to synchronize your iTunes folder and the external drive's version.

Restoring from a backup

If the worst happens and you need to restore your backup, simply drag the folder back into its original location, overwriting the original if necessary. If, when you open iTunes, this hasn't done the trick, open iTunes Preferences, click the Advanced button and then Change… to point iTunes to the folder.

Back up to CDs or DVDs

iTunes includes a useful tool for backing up your files and playlists to CDs or DVDs. With this technique, expect to fit around 150–200 tracks on a CD and around 750–1000 on a DVD. Note, though, that these discs won't be playable on regular CD or DVD players.

Getting started

To open the iTunes back-up tool, click the Back Up to Disc option in the File > Library menu. Next choose whether you want to back up your entire collection, complete with playlists, or just the songs you've downloaded from the iTunes Store (the idea being that any other songs you already have backed up on the original CDs).

Next, press Back Up and iTunes will prompt you to insert a disc. If that one gets filled up, it will ask for more.

Subsequent backups

To update your backup, you can either do the same thing again on new discs. Or, if you want to save time and discs, check the box to only back up items added or changed since your last backup.

Welcome to iTunes Backup

Back up your iTunes library to CDs or DVDs.

⦿ Back up entire iTunes library and playlists

◯ Back up only iTunes Store purchases

☐ Only back up items added or changed since last backup

Restoring from a backup

To restore your backed-up iTunes collection, simply open iTunes and insert the first of the backup CDs or DVDs. iTunes will take care of the rest.

Backing up to a remote server

If you have a Web hosting account or are a .Mac member, you could instead choose to back up to a remote server. For a standard Web hosting account, use an FTP program to upload the iTunes folder up to your Web space. For .Mac, use the Backup tool that comes free with all accounts.

iPod as back-up device

If you enable your iPod as a hard drive (see p.190), then you can use it to back up all types of documents and other files. Applications such as Jax (see p.238) can even automate the process each time you connect your Pod.

iPod touch backups

Every time you sync an iPod touch, a special backup file is created, containing details of apps, settings, any notes you may have written, map bookmarks, etc. These backups can be found listed for any iPod touch (or iPhone), used in conjunction with iTunes, within iTunes Preferences under the Devices tab.

You can manually force iTunes to update the backup of an iPod touch by right-clicking the device's icon in the Sources sidebar and choosing Back Up.

If you ever need to transfer settings to a new iPod touch, or reinstall settings after restoring an iPod touch (see p.252) you can utilize the relevent backup by right-clicking the iPod's icon in the Sources sidebar and choosing Restore from Backup…

Devices							
General	Playback	Sharing	Store	Parental	Apple TV	Devices	Advanced

Device backups:

Castorp	Yesterday 16:46
Parsley	Yesterday 17:47
Rosalie's iPod Touch	Today 12:33

☐ Disable automatic syncing for iPhones and iPods   (Delete Backup)

☑ Look for remote speakers connected with AirTunes
   ☐ Disable iTunes volume control for remote speakers
   ☐ Allow iTunes control from remote speakers
☑ Look for iPhone and iPod Touch Remotes   (Forget All Remotes)

(Cancel)   (OK)

27

Help!

Troubleshooting & maintenance

Despite the minimalist design of the iPod, and the intuitive look and feel of iTunes, both can throw the occasional curve-ball. There are a million and one things that might be the cause of your woes – and we don't have the space to cover all of them here. However, this chapter does provide answers to the most common iPod and iTunes problems – as well as tips on maximizing your iPod's battery life. As for the rest, there's always the Internet, so if you don't find the help you need here, turn to p.261 for a couple more online resources.

iPod ailments

General troubleshooting: reset, update, restore

Just like regular computers, iPods sometimes crash, freeze up, or generally start behaving like belligerent two-year-olds. This is usually a software glitch and can generally be solved by resetting, updating or restoring the iPod…

Resetting an iPod

Resetting your iPod basically means rebooting it. Songs and other contents won't be affected. Here's how its done:

▶ **Post-2004 iPods (classic, nano, video, mini)** Hold down Menu & Select until the Apple logo appears.

▶ **iPod touch** Press and hold the Sleep/Wake button and the Home button at the same time for around ten seconds.

▶ **iPod shuffle** Turn off for 5 seconds and then turn back on.

▶ **Older iPods** Hold down ▶II & Menu until the Apple logo appears.

If this doesn't have any effect, try connecting the Pod to its power supply, toggling the Hold switch, and then resetting again.

> **TIP:** Also try resetting the preferences of an iPod touch. All settings will be lost, but no data deleted. Tap Settings > General > Reset >Reset All Settings.

Updating

If resetting doesn't solve the problem, try updating the iPod's internal software. Open iTunes, connect the iPod and click Check for Updates. If an update is on offer, install it. Software updates are generally free, though touch users are sometimes asked to pay a small fee when a major update with new features is released.

Restoring

If updating doesn't solve the problem, use the Restore button to
return the Pod to its factory state. Be warned, however, that this
will completely blank the iPod so you'll need to wait for iTunes to
refill it afterwards. If you use your iPod as a hard drive, be sure to
copy any essential files to your computer before restoring.

My iPod doesn't appear when I plug it in

Try resetting and updating the iPod, as described, above. If that
doesn't work, try the following steps and, if necessary, restore the
iPod to factory settings.

▶ **Empty your Trash and restart your computer** A software
glitch or a full hard drive can stop Mac OS X recognizing attached
drives.

▶ **Force-mount** If iTunes sees the iPod but it won't work as a hard
drive, even though Disk Use is enabled (see p.190), try resetting the
Pod and, when the Apple logo appears, holding down Select and ▶ll
(recent iPods) or l◀◀ and ▶▶l (older models) to force it into Disk Mode.

▶ **Delete iPodDriver.kext** On a Mac, search for a file of this name
and, if you find it, delete it.

Reading the iPod shuffle's lights

Because the iPod shuffle has no screen, it communicates via its little flashing light.
Here's how to interpret what it's trying to say:

▶ **Red when you turn it on** Very low battery charge.

▶ **Continuous orange blink** Do not disconnect from computer.

▶ **Green/orange two-second blink** There is no loaded music.

▶ **Green/orange/orange ten-second blink** The firmware is damaged and the
iPod needs to be restored.

The display is in the wrong language

To get back to English on a click-wheel iPod, first hit the Menu button a few times to reach the top-level. Then select the second item from the bottom – this is always Settings. In the next menu, select the third item up (always Language) and choose English.

Look online...

If your Pod is still not behaving – and you've tried everything obvious, such as plugging it in to recharge and making sure the Hold switch isn't on (see p.50), then search online for help. Search Google, check the iPod sites listed in Chapter 26 and, if you're still struggling, pose a question at discussions.apple.com.

Sending an iPod for repair

If all else fails, you'll need to send your Pod to meet its maker. Repair can be arranged via an Apple retail store, but you may have to make an appointment in advance. Alternatively, Apple will mail you a box in which you can post the Pod back to them. You can arrange this at depot.info.apple.com/ipod or by calling 1-800/275-2273 (US) or 0870 8760 753 (UK). Either way, you'll need to provide your Pod's serial number, which you'll find on the back of the device in tiny print.

Diagnostic mode

It is possible to run various tests on a click-wheel iPod in Diagnostic Mode, which is entered by resetting the Pod and then, when the Apple logo appears, pressing |◀◀, ▶▶| and **Select** (on older iPod models) or pressing |◀◀ and **Select** (on newer models) until you hear a little chirp, at which point a new menu should appear. The tests are very techie, and not really designed for consumer use. So if you do want to explore this mode, be sure to read up on the subject online before you start. A good place to start is *ipoding.com*.

Battery issues

The controversy surrounding the iPod battery is largely in the past (see p.16), but it's still worth bearing the following in mind to maximize the performance and longevity of the iPod battery.

To maximize the battery life from each charge

▶ **Keep your iPod software up to date** See p.251.

▶ **Use the Hold switch** so that your iPod doesn't sing to itself in your pocket when buttons get pressed accidentally.

▶ **Stay lo-fi** Avoid super-high-quality song files as these take more processing power to play back.

▶ **Let it play** Try not to use the I◄◄, **Select** and ►►I buttons too frequently on iPod classics (and other iPod models with a hard-drive rather than flash memory), as they require extra hard-drive access.

▶ **Minimize backlight use** Only illuminate the screen when you really need to.

To extend the battery's overall life span

▶ **Plug it in when not in use** It's a myth that you should run down your battery completely before each charge. In truth, this seriously harms the overall lifespan. However, you *should* let it run down completely once a month or thereabouts.

▶ **Use your iPod regularly** Extended periods of inactivity don't do the battery any good.

▶**Avoid extreme temperatures** The battery will perform best and last longest if usually kept near room temperature. Avoid direct sunlight and sub-freezing temperatures.

Replacing the battery

If your iPod battery does eventually run out of steam, you could send the Pod to Apple for a replacement. This will be free if your warranty hasn't expired or, more likely, $59/£49 plus shipping. For more information, see:

Service & Support apple.com/support/ipod

Alternatively, you could opt for a less expensive service via a third-party company, or even buy a battery kit for as little as $15/£10 and fit it yourself. Explore the following:

iPodBattery.com ipodbattery.com (US)
iPodResQ ipodresq.com (US)
iPod Doctor ipoddoctor.co.uk (UK)

iTunes Problems

If iTunes is playing up, the first thing to try is downloading and installing the latest version (see p.40).

Out of disk space

First, tidy up your music and video collection. Remove any duplicates in iTunes (see p.150), consolidate your Library, and then delete files strewn across your computer (see p.58), and consider converting any bulky AIFF, WAV or Apple Lossless files to a compressed format (see p.66). To locate bulky files, try sorting your songs by file size (see p.127).

Next look at your system as a whole and see if you can save any space by deleting, or archiving, old files and disposing of temporary files. Finally, empty the trash. If you still don't have enough space, invest in an extra hard drive (see p.246).

The text in my Song List looks garbled

This could be a problem with your ID3 tags – the code that stores the track info. Try selecting the track or tracks and choosing Convert ID3 Tags… from the iTunes Advanced menu.

iTunes says my Library file is invalid

If you've recently moved your iTunes folder or Library file, point iTunes to the new location, as described on p.153. If not, it could be that the Library file (which stores data such as playlists, play counts, etc) has become corrupt.

In this case, you could try replacing it with a backed-up version, if you ever made one. If not, you could try using an iPod-to-iTunes copying tools (see p.236) to restore the information from your iPod to iTunes. Or, if you don't mind losing the playlists, ratings and so on, try dragging your iTunes Music folder (see p.153) into the main iTunes window to reimport the music and video.

Dead computers & iPods

If your computer dies or gets stolen, you can either restore your collection to a new PC or Mac from a backup, if you made one (see p.247), or download a program to copy everything over from your iPod (see p.236). Whatever you do, don't sync your iPod with the new, empty copy of iTunes – you'll lose everything.

If you upgrade your computer, the same options apply. Or you could copy the files from the old computer to the new one as described on p.90.

As for iPods, if you have one that is no longer worth saving, be sure to send it to Apple – or take it to an Apple Store – for recycling. In the US, this will get you a ten percent discount on a new model. See apple.com/environment/recycling for more information.

iPodology

28

iPods online

Websites and blogs

I f you want to find out more about any of the subjects covered in this book – or track down that elusive iPod accessory, join a forum or download the latest iTunes plug-ins – you're going to have to hit the Web. There's an almost frightening number of iPod and iTunes sites out there, including comprehensive Pod portals, with discussion forums, troubleshooting tips, news and reviews. Apple's own site is also a useful resource, and there are even a number of iPod blogs (weblogs). Following are the pick of the bunch; for online Pod weirdness, turn to p.263.

iPod sites & forums

iLounge ilounge.com
iPodObserver ipodobserver.com
iPodSites Directory ipodsites.com
iProng iprong.com
Touch Arcade toucharcade.com

Apple

Home apple.com
iTunes/iPod home apple.com/itunes
Apple Store apple.com/store
Apple Discussions discussions.apple.com
Software Updates apple.com/support/downloads
Service & Support apple.com/support/ipod

Help, hacks & maintenance

iPod Hacks ipodhacks.com
MacFixit macfixit.com

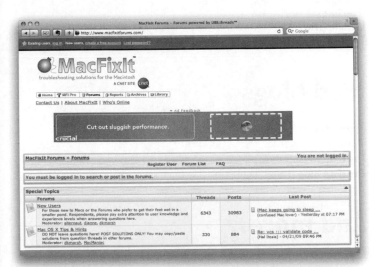

Buying & accessories

Amazon amazon.com
Apple Store apple.com/store
Belkin belkin.com
Everything iPod everythingipod.com
Griffin griffintechnology.com
iLounge ilounge.com/loungestore.php

Software downloads

About macs.about.com/cs/itunes/a/itunes_utils.htm
Doug's AppleScripts dougscripts.com/itunes
iLounge ilounge.com/downloads.php
iPodSoft ipodsoft.com
LittleAppFactory thelittleappfactory.com
TuCows tucows.com

iPod blogs

Apple iPhone & iPod Blog appleiphoneandipod.blogspot.com
iPoding ipoding.com
The iPod Nation theipodnation.com
The iPod Blog theipodblog.com

And more…

For an overview of what the iPod is, who made it happen and how it's changed over the years, visit the relevant pages of Wikipedia, starting with:

Wikipedia en.wikipedia.org/wiki/IPod

If you have a suggestion about how the iPod could be improved, then tell Apple at:

iPod Feedback apple.com/feedback/ipod.html

29

iP*odd*

Stranger than fiction

I t is, without a doubt, a weird world, and there's nothing quite like music, gadgets and fads to bring the crackpots out of the woodwork. What follows are a few dispatches from the people who put the odd in the Pod.

Engravings from hell

What not to get engraved on your little shiny friend:

ipodlaughs.com/ipod/iengraver
methodshop.com/mp3/articles/iPodEngraving
ipodlaughs.com/ipod/ipocalypse/disturbingengravings.asp

And, if you want the T-shirt, visit…

cafeshops.com/ipod_laughs

Linux on iPod

Bored of playing music? Why not use your iPod as a platform for a UNIX-clone operating system?

iPod health warnings

Love your Pod a little too much? Be cured here:

theregister.co.uk/2005/05/20/ipod_health_warnings/

Photo galleries

What do you get if you cross an iPod with Photoshop?

ipodlaughs.com/ipod/ipocalypse

And for shots of globetrotting Pods:

gallery.ilounge.com

A close shave...

A hoax, perhaps, but also one of the best ideas since sliced bread.

Apple-ad-meets-Microsoft-man magic moment

Pod users who have seen the widely circulated videos of
Microsoft's Steve Ballmer (ntk.net/ballmer) will love this reworking:

macboy.com/cartoons/ballmer

iPod open mic

This London club-night invites you to bring your own music –
fifteen minutes on stage to show what your Pod can do…

Playlist ipod-dj.com

iPod app weirdness

The iPod touch has now become
the torch-carrier of all things
wacky in iPod Land thanks to the
App Store, and some of the truly
outlandish stuff that is on offer.
Among our favourites are:

Annoyance Annoying sounds at your
fingertips.
Cow Toss Let's you toss a virtual cow.
You'll wonder how you managed to
live without it.
Awesome Ball It is what it is.
i2D2 The droid you can keep in your
pocket (pictured).

iGod

Or if you prefer divine inspiration to club perspiration, you're
going to need this:

BiblePod kainjow.com/?xml/software/biblepod.xml

Pod DIY

If money is an issue, there are always
the rather special paper iPod alternatives,
which can be found at
homepage.mac.com/colinbaxter/ipod/ipodclick.html

From sickjokes.net, here's a very
easy way to transform your iPod
into an iPod shuffle, using only a
humble Post-it note.

TIP: If you don't like the backlight colour of your
iPod's screen and, on third-generation models,
the buttons – and you don't mind voiding your warranty – try
something in blue, green or orange. Visit ipodmods.com

Check this out... gizmodo.com/images/bizzaro_ipod.mov

Dock crazy

Is it a bird? Is it a plane? No, it's a log ...
with legs and speakers and an iPod dock
up-top.

Storylog
housespecial.org/
products/
storylog.htm

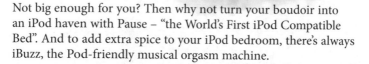

Not big enough for you? Then why not turn your boudoir into
an iPod haven with Pause – "the World's First iPod Compatible
Bed". And to add extra spice to your iPod bedroom, there's always
iBuzz, the Pod-friendly musical orgasm machine.

Pause designmobel.co.nz/pause.html
iBuzz ibuzz.co.uk

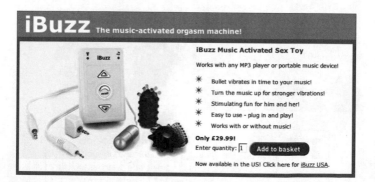

iPod-megaphone-helmet

Great for selling ice-cream and more likely to get you noticed at a party than turning up with an Apple iPod Hi-Fi (see p.232). For full instructions on how to pimp your own helmet, visit: instructables.com

Fancy dress

iPod fancy dress can be approached from both directions – either you dress up (right), or your Pod does (below) with a nifty little case from Shanalogic.

Shanalogic shanalogic.com

Larry Koteff made this wonderful iPod costume in 2003.

Bricking it

Who needs a Dock when all the raw materials are sitting at the back of the toy cupboard?

flickr.com/photos/linuxmatt/sets

In fact, who needs an iPod at all when you have Lego?

PodBrix podbrix.com

Here's one we made earlier...

Index

Index

index

index

index

index